Praise for

Where Did You Get This Number?

"Salvanto's explanations and real-world examples add nuance to the numbers and graphs that fill the news. General interest readers and news junkies alike will come away with a greater appreciation of how polls and surveys are conducted, as well as a much clearer sense of what they mean."

—Publishers Weekly

"Anthony Salvanto has written a good book about polling, and you had better read it if you want to understand how professionals go about getting the right readings as they take the temperature of our country."

—Peggy Noonan, Pulitzer Prize–winning columnist,
The Wall Street Journal

"Mr. Salvanto . . . explains matters well known to political junkies: how samples are weighted to reflect relevant characteristics of the expected electorate; how questions are worded to avoid nudging respondents in one direction or another; how a random sample of 1,000 people can almost always provide a usefully close approximation of the opinions of tens of millions. . . . If you want to get a feel for what it's like working at a network decision desk on election night, go read Mr. Salvanto's first chapter."

—The Wall Street Journal

"In his new book *Where Did You Get This Number?*, Salvanto begins on election night [2016], the events of which surprised him less than they did most Americans. He proceeds, in digestible and timely fashion, to demystify the world of polling and pollsters."

—The Guardian

Where Did You Get This Number?

A Pollster's Guide to Making Sense of the World

Anthony Salvanto

Simon & Schuster Paperbacks

New York   London   Toronto   Sydney   New Delhi

To Aidan and Theo

Simon & Schuster Paperbacks
An Imprint of Simon & Schuster, Inc.
1230 Avenue of the Americas
New York, NY 10020

First Simon & Schuster trade paperback edition August 2019

SIMON & SCHUSTER PAPERBACKS and colophon are registered trademarks of
Simon & Schuster, Inc.

For information about special discounts for bulk purchases, please contact
Simon & Schuster Special Sales at 1-866-506-1949 or business@simonandschuster.com.

The Simon & Schuster Speakers Bureau can bring authors to your live event. For
more information, or to book an event, contact the Simon & Schuster Speakers
Bureau at 1-866-248-3049 or visit our website at www.simonspeakers.com.

Interior design by Ruth Lee-Mui

Manufactured in the United States of America

10 9 8 7 6 5 4 3 2 1

Library of Congress Cataloging-in-Publication Data is available.

ISBN 978-1-5011-7483-4
ISBN 978-1-5011-7485-8 (pbk)
ISBN 978-1-5011-7484-1 (ebook)

Contents

Where Did You Get This Number?

Chapter One

The Seen and the Unseen

At 2:52 a.m. on Election Night at the CBS News Decision Desk, I reached for the intercom button with my left hand and told the broadcast's control room we were ready.

What had once seemed unlikely was now certain.

I was staring at big monitors filled with numbers, at vote reports coming in from Pennsylvania: the polls had closed seven hours ago and Donald Trump and Hillary Clinton were still less than a point apart. We weren't really sure those reports were finished, but now we knew we'd seen *enough* of them; enough to know for sure what was happening.

Figuring out just what *enough* is, that's always the hard part on nights like this.

With my right hand I pulled up a small menu on the screen and then a little gray box that's been deliberately tucked away, in a spot where it can only be pushed on purpose. It has the "W" in it—for "Win."

"We're calling Pennsylvania for Trump," I said into the headset. My click signaled graphics to light up the state in red on the big U.S. map, it sent the state's electoral votes over into the Republican column, and pushed Trump's count over the 270 he needed—which is why we'd been so focused on Pennsylvania for the last hour. I need to be right on every call, but I *really* need to be right on the one that decides everything. ". . . and projecting the presidency with it," I followed. "Donald Trump, elected."

The name "Decision Desk" is newsroom slang for what's really a long U-shaped set of tables behind the anchors here in CBS's Studio 57, the hub of our Election Night coverage. If you watch the show you can see those tables stacked with computers and the monitors that we're squinting at all night, as data feeds stream in with vote results from every corner of the country. There's a big lighted sign hanging over it that reads "Decision" and from here my small cadre of pollsters and professors and I call the races for the network: who's leading, who's trailing, who wins, and who loses across fifty states, hundreds of contests, 130 million votes. There were times in past years when the Desk was hidden out of sight in a different room with no cameras—let alone any big lighted signs—and known only by its proclamations of who won. But I love that we're out here in the main studio where the viewers can see and hear from us as the night rolls along. These are, after all, their votes we're looking at.

In Studio 57 there is no offstage: the anchors sit at a round glass table in the center; there are producers around the perimeter typing and talking softly but urgently; robotic cameras whirling remotely and black-clad cameramen with Steadicams pointing from place to place; giant screens, floor to ceiling, are alight with the red and blue vote map; live streams with remote views of cheering crowds at some campaign headquarters and sunken faces at others; displays flashing Twitter feeds scrolling past too fast to read.

For eight straight hours that had all been a swirl of kinetic energy but now, at this moment, nearly 3 a.m. and the presidency decided, it slows a bit and the focus shifts elsewhere: Donald Trump is at a podium in New York addressing his supporters.

I took off the headset and stepped back from the desk. After we call a presidential race, I always try to take a moment and recognize the history we've just seen, whoever wins. On the exposed-brick wall next to us, the set designers had laid out old tchotchkes, campaign memorabilia, photos, all juxtaposed against our technology and those screens, reminders that the Decision Desk has a great history of its own. I have one shot of Walter Cronkite in 1968 in front of a board showing Richard Nixon's and Hubert Humphrey's vote counts; right next to my seat is another black-and-white photo of pinstripe-suited CBS staffers in the 1950s frantically tallying votes in chalk on a big blackboard. These are the traditions we follow even as the politics and the technology change through the years. The dress codes change, too, it occurs to me: those guys in the photo are still dutifully wearing their suits even amid the chalk smears, and at this point I'm in rolled-up shirtsleeves, jacket off, tie down. I just pull the tie back up when I go on camera beside that big touchscreen to explain what's going on—which I'd done more of on this night than any before.

Tomorrow would be busy for me, too. Everyone would be trying to understand how Donald Trump had defied the expectations: the ones set by the pundits, the forecasters, and some—though hardly all—of the polls. We'd just seen some of the answers as all those votes had poured in. At the Decision Desk, our job is to show you what's happening when you can't see everything; when you don't know every vote, or every county, or every person. But the numbers and the winners we light up are just the attention-grabbing parts at the end. The real discoveries come in trying to figure those numbers out in the first place.

This story begins with how we do that on Election Nights, and what this very late, very close one showed us.

Sunday, November 6, two days before Election Day

Two days earlier, on the weekend before Election Day, we'd gathered in the studio to rehearse scenarios that might unfold that Tuesday night, kicking around ideas of what we'd need to see to make a call in every state, and what we'd say on air in each instance. We'd run all the anchors and producers through scenarios for both a Trump win and a Clinton win; what states might flip, what the timing might look like in either case.

In the newsroom someone asked me as we worked through the Trump scenario: "Why does *The New York Times* say Clinton is going to win?" The *Times* wasn't actually declaring her a winner at that point, of course. But the forecasts running on the paper's website, which were trying to predict the contest in advance, did seem to us to be overconfident in Clinton, offering up assessments of her chances that most people would mistakenly interpret as certainties. On our *Face the Nation* program that Sunday, we'd released our own final round of pre-election polls from the states of Ohio and Florida showing they were moving in Trump's direction. The national polls also had him closing the gap. And if all that was moving, other states we hadn't polled might be changing, as well. It couldn't be ruled out.

I'd run into our chief White House correspondent, Major Garrett, a few days before that in the Green Room, the waiting area before we went on *CBS This Morning*. Major had spent the year covering the Trump campaign. I was planning to go on and describe a tough-but-doable Electoral College path for Trump that ran through the states of the Upper Midwest (which later turned out to be the one he took) or maybe Colorado (which he didn't). I'd been describing Trump as "down, but not out." I started bouncing that idea off Major, but he beat me to it. "He could win," he said emphatically, noting the size and enthusiasm of Trump crowds he'd seen in every venue at every hour of the day. I nodded. Neither of us thought that meant Trump *would* win, but we agreed the possibility was there.

12:00 Noon, Election Day, Midtown Manhattan

My Election Day began well away from the Broadcast Center and the Decision Desk. Fifteen hours before I made that call for Trump, long before the studio heated up and we started the broadcast, I'd gotten to see an early indicator of what might happen. Just after noon I'd gone into the TV networks' Quarantine room, at an undisclosed location in Manhattan—essentially a borrowed, nondescript office space with no windows—where a handful of representatives from each of the participating networks can go to privately see early exit poll data while voting is still going on, hours before it will be made public.

The exit polls are the first way we get a look at what's unfolding on Election Day. Thousands of interviewers had fanned out across the country from the opening of voting places that morning, some in place by 6 a.m., heading out on behalf of the TV networks to thousands of precincts. They were handing out questionnaires to voters leaving those polling places: single sheets of paper with large-type font, our TV logos printed across the top along with "CONFIDENTIAL" in capital letters, and a handful of questions arrayed below like "In today's election for President did you just vote for:" then checkboxes along with the candidates' names, and "When did you finally decide for whom to vote?"

"What was most important in your decision?" and all ending with bold-faced instructions to fold the paper and drop it in a box. When all was said and done they'd collect more than 100,000 of these questionnaires.

At this point in the afternoon, those interviews with voters had just begun. The interviewers transmitted the first set of the morning's initial data from the interviews, then went back and kept interviewing. My counterparts at the other networks and I all want to see those first reports to get a jump on preparing stories, but because they're so preliminary, and because people are still voting across the country, we need to make it as private as possible. So it's only piped into the Quarantine room (dubbed the "Q-room" for short) where there are no Internet ports, no Wi-Fi, and as you enter you turn in all your electronics to a guard at the door, and agree that you can't leave until 5 p.m. You even get escorted to the bathroom down the hall, complete with our it-doesn't-get-old joke that someone who wanted to leak the numbers might hide a cell phone behind the toilet, like Michael Corleone with the gun in *The Godfather*.

Sitting in the Quarantine room, in my read of the morning's data, the presidential contest was effectively even. That first round of data suggested Clinton was up, but only narrowly at best, and there was plenty of reason to think the trend was moving toward Trump as the voting went on that afternoon. The question was whether it would keep moving, in enough places, and I suspected it could. Through the afternoon those exit polls are incomplete. Millions of people still had yet to cast ballots and the voting was still open everywhere. The trick for us is to figure out who's still left out there to vote, who it is we're *not* seeing yet among our interviews; which kinds of voters might show up later that night, or who might have even just skipped taking the poll altogether.

I ran some comparisons against the precincts, and noticed people who might still vote were older, whiter, and working-class: just the kind of voters Trump was going after.

The first task in calling races is knowing the difference between the seen and the unseen. If what we're looking at any moment—in this case, those first exit polls—could be different from the rest of them, we wait. We don't know the whole story yet.

I left the Quarantine room after 5 p.m. and made my way across town to the Broadcast Center. When I got there at 5:30 all the producers and anchors had gathered in the conference room for a quick briefing as we prepared to go on the air live. "This," I told everyone, "is a contested race." And I told them to get set for a very late night.

That much, at least, I was sure about.

7:30 p.m., CBS Decision Desk, Studio 57

The show is on the air now. The big U.S. map waits to be filled in, state by state, with red and blue for the winners as we call them.

When I was a kid I remember staying up late in front of the TV on Election Nights like this, but I didn't watch for the politics, at least not at first. I was initially drawn in because I liked sports, and to me all this was being presented in the same sort of way as a big game. They showed stats and numbers on the screen, that U.S. map like a scoreboard; there were winners and losers, and it all looked like the Super Bowl of Serious Things. I remember thinking it was cool that it all happened despite its enormous, national scope—in fact, it was amazing *because* of its scope.

As it turned out, I was wrong about Election Night being like sports.

A game unfolds play by play, and events and scores come sequentially until time's up. But tune in on Election Night and you're watching the results from events that are *over*. When we talk about a state, the polls have closed there, all the ballots are sitting in bins or a counting machine and so the result—the voters' choice—is final. It's just that nobody knows what it is yet.

It'll emerge as a mosaic of reports that fill in across the country slowly and randomly, never the same way every year. Voting in the United States is run at the local and state level, and everyone's little portion of those 130 million votes is, by and large, counted somewhere close to *you*, with each town or county or state going at its own pace. Knowing that's going to happen means we try to get a sense of the whole picture from those tiny pieces as they pop up one by one. We look for patterns, commonalities in what's emerging. We're not predicting what will be, we're revealing a story about what *is*. And my job now, on these nights, is to assemble that picture as fast as I can and relay it to you. That's part of the tradition we carry, too.

And because there's a kid out there somewhere whose parents are telling him to go to bed.

The voting closes in North Carolina, a battleground both campaigns are contesting hard, but exactly what's happening there is uncertain. I look at the statistical models on our screens and they show Clinton is up as the first reports arrive, with a sizable edge, but one we don't suspect will hold up. These first tallies we're seeing are from absentee ballots, which were mailed in and dropped off days or weeks ago. They've probably been sitting around, queued up first for the tabulating machines at county offices. If they're first to get counted, they'll be first to get reported now. From the television screens around the studio, we overhear our reporters at campaign headquarters say the Clinton campaign is confident about them because absentee voters tend to vote more Democratic, are a little younger, but working jobs with shifts and less flexible hours. I'd heard people describing Clinton as having "votes already in the bank" heading into tonight because of that. Meanwhile, though, the exit poll interviews from this afternoon tell us Trump did better with the voters who'd shown up to cast ballots today, and when their votes get counted, we figure Trump could make that Clinton edge shrink, or even disappear. It's that race caller's—and pollster's—rule again: if what you're looking at right now could be different from everything else, be careful.

Sure enough, within the hour, our models show Clinton's lead down to two points and shrinking, her "votes in the bank" being quickly devalued as Trump starts to overtake her. Clinton would ultimately lose the state, her edge in advance votes not enough to offset Trump's turnout surge on Election Day. In the counties where Trump was doing best, turnout was running almost even with what we'd expected, and sometimes higher. In the ones Clinton was carrying, turnout was just a shade *under* expectations. That, it turned out, was another sign, the start of a pattern we'd need to remember later.

7:58 p.m.

The broadcast gets set to return from a commercial break and the control room asks me for the "top of the hour" rundown: how we'll characterize the races in states where voting closes in two minutes, at eight o'clock.

Nancy Cordes, our correspondent who's been traveling with the Clinton campaign, is at the Javits Center in New York City amid a huge crowd clearly expecting to celebrate a presidential win in a few hours.

Nancy reports that the Clinton campaign says they feel very good now about Florida, one of those eight o'clock states, in particular because of Miami and the Hispanic vote there. Another of the assumptions heading into the night was that Hispanic voters would propel Clinton across the fast-growing states of the Sun Belt.

At the Desk, what I see is a different—and bigger—picture.

I tell the control room we'll describe Florida as a pure toss-up at 8:00, not a Clinton lead. While she is indeed doing well in Miami (it'll turn out later that she does better than Obama did there). Miami is not a barometer. In fact, no single place is. All our state estimates on Election

Night have to take into account everything we can see from all over the state, not just a key county or two—and right now it looks like Clinton is getting beaten most everywhere else in Florida.

8:45 p.m.

We're starting to light up that U.S. map in red and blue now. We've made a string of easier calls in lopsided, partisan states: Trump picks up Alabama and Tennessee. Clinton strings some together in the Mid-Atlantic: Delaware, Maryland, and New Jersey.

At the Desk we blend a range of expertise and we divide up the roles. Statisticians Doug Rivers and Delia Bailey spend much of this night looking for patterns across precincts; Mark Gersh, who does congressional campaign strategy for a living, sits with a red Alabama cap perpetually pulled down to his eyebrows, staring at a long sheet of graph paper with vote numbers printed on it—which I think is just a refresher course for him, because he's somehow managed to memorize the vote history of every county in America. Steve Ansolabehere knows all the voting systems and David Winston knows key states like Ohio inside out. There are Democrats and Republicans here, but one wouldn't know it from the discussions. To all of us this night is the same puzzle to solve. The campaigning is over, anyway. My rule, handed down to me from my predecessors, is that everyone needs to agree before we call a race. Our vice president of news standards, Al Ortiz, keeps tabs on what we report, and from time to time the president of CBS News, David Rhodes, swings by, and they ask when we can make a call, but without pressure, and it's just too early to say.

Seated next to me is Murray Edelman, a consultant for us now, but who more than forty years ago helped build the foundation of how we do things today.

Back when networks began competing to call races in earnest in the 1950s and 1960s, computers—which, Murray reminds me, were so big at the time they could take up an entire room and were fed by punch cards—had come along with advances in statistics that made it both alluring and possible to quickly figure out what was happening on Election Night. The networks were taking up the challenge. They'd even take out full-page ads in the newspapers the day after an election for bragging rights. I have one that lists a long string of vote estimates from every state—in tiny, eight-point type, each down to the decimal point—that their big computers had spit out the night before.

Edelman was a young graduate student in 1967, recruited along with CBS's new elections head, Warren Mitofsky, beginning an era of innovations that would become legendary in the polling world. Even if I hadn't seen Murray's yellowed notebooks from the era, with his handwritten formulas on them, one could tell that so many of our techniques began as his creations, just from the way he describes computations as we test them out, how they'll get better or worse with every new update, like a parent who knows what will set off or soothe their kid's moods.

They made sure every precinct in the state had the chance to be included in the models that they watched on Election Night, the ones that show the story—in number form—of what's emerging. They divided a state into four or five regions and waited for votes from every one of them, like buckets that had to fill up, so that a Decision Desk could know it was accounting for every part and every place. It became a cornerstone of the modern approach. Nowadays, the precincts for exit polls are still picked at random every year; our interviewers go to big places and small ones, to country and city precincts, Democratic-leaning places, Republican-leaning places, and everything in between. No place is picked for an exit poll, or discarded for that matter, just because of how we assume it'll vote. Because we never know in advance where the big vote shifts might occur, and surprises are the last thing you want.

This is also why I cringe a little when I still hear people point to spots and say things like "watch this little town that always votes for the winner." The key to any good poll is quite the opposite of that: it's making sure that *everyone* gets represented.

9:00 p.m.

We call Kansas for Trump the moment its polls close. Both Michigan and Wisconsin close and, ominously for Clinton, we see tight races, nothing even statistically close to being a "call." These were both states she'd been expected to win.

The exit polls start telling more of their story, too. The interviewers talk to voters until the voting ends, then they go in and talk to election officials, as well, and get the official precinct results straight from them. We update our models with the counts from the officials, and the small leads Clinton had in some areas of Michigan and Wisconsin shrink even further.

10:00 p.m.

It was sometime around the 10:00 mark that I think the idea of this whole race as a complete toss-up, and perhaps a Trump win, really emerged for the campaigns the same way it had appeared to us at the Desk early on. Major Garrett, reporting from Trump headquarters, says that while earlier this evening there was despondency, now there's a cautious optimism. From the anchor table, Norah O'Donnell says to viewers, "If you're a Clinton supporter you're popping an anti-anxiety pill right now."

The votes have been coming in from Michigan for an hour now, and our estimates put Trump up there by two. By this time of night, in

2012 or 2008, Michigan had shown a wide lead for Democrats. When the Trump campaign said during the year they'd contest Michigan, they'd drawn some derision. But like a lot of the Upper Midwest, it's got a higher share of working-class voters now propelling him. John Dickerson, one of our anchors, notes that four years earlier, I'd called not only Michigan much earlier, but Pennsylvania, too, for Democrats. Obama had been well on his way, cruising through states that always voted Democratic. Not so for Clinton tonight.

There's an even more recent comparison that catches my eye. I look at Michigan's and Wisconsin's county maps, where each county was colored in for the candidate ahead in it, now that we've got more votes to look at. The pattern looked familiar, like the county maps we had seen that spring, on primary nights, in the Democratic contest between Clinton and her rival for the nomination, Bernie Sanders. Back in the springtime, in those primary races in Michigan and Wisconsin, Clinton had done relatively well in the cities like Milwaukee and Detroit, and Sanders had done well everywhere else—in the outer suburbs, the rural counties. Now in November, on this Election Night, the urban counties were lit again for Clinton, but once again the vast landscape beyond them was lit for her opponent—this time, for Trump. I wondered if that was a holdover, a story unfolding in county map form: out in those rural areas, maybe there were Democrats who never did get past a primary loss for Sanders, deciding to sit this one out.

No one yells at anyone at the Decision Desk; at least not at ours. It's not like on dramatic shows and in movies about newsrooms where these kinds of nights are portrayed with shouting and people running around, demanding some race be called or not. For one thing, there's a live broadcast happening ten feet away and sometimes we've been reminded to hush, but it's mostly because the language we use has to be in methodical, operating-room style. There's no other way to get through it all.

We start looking at Ohio, and whether we can make a call for Trump.

David Winston says: "Franklin County is reporting now. It's sixty-four percent Clinton."

Murray Edelman asks: "Any change to the models?" He wants to know if that report changes the overall leader in our estimates of the race, or is it what we'd expected to see in Franklin County, anyhow.

Gersh is already looking and chimes in: "No."

I ask: "How does the size look?" "Size" is shorthand for turnout, the size of a county expressed in vote terms. This also becomes a check on the quality of our data. If there's anything out of the ordinary from a county, such as a far bigger or smaller turnout than ever before, like twenty thousand votes reported in a place that holds two hundred people, the system will put up a warning flag, and we'll want to double-check it.

Doug Rivers: "It's the same as expected."

We always use the past vote in a county for Democrats and Republicans as a benchmark for comparison to the moment. The fact that we can do this tells a political story in itself: so many voters are so consistently partisan, that a comparison allows us to pick up a shift in votes that can be telling. In most every state, red or blue, we find cities tend to be more Democratic and Republicans do better in suburban and more rural areas farther out, but it's how *much* better or worse they're doing tonight that matters. A Republican getting 55 percent in counties where Republicans usually get 50 percent is having a good night. A Democrat getting 60 percent in places Democrats usually get 70 is having a bad one.

As we head toward 10:30, Ohio becomes an example of calling a race off a pattern that's emerging, long before we see all of its votes. In county after county, mostly in smaller rural ones, we see Trump doing better than other recent Republican candidates have done, beating the Republican benchmarks. Winston is keeping an eye on it now and it's getting close to a "computational call" status, he says, which means we think vote trends we're seeing are so widespread, not relegated to just a few places, that they can't be idiosyncratic. Something real is happening.

With about three-quarters of the vote in from Ohio, Clinton is running ahead of a typical Democrat in only six of eighty-eight counties. Trump is ahead of usual Republican benchmarks in all the others, and up in them by ten points on average. We apply that key test: is what we're seeing so far telling us enough about the whole of the state? Watching all these counties moving toward Trump, one after another, gives us confidence that it is.

I tell the control room we're at "likely" status to call the race, but stand by, there's still one last thing to check. Trump is winning in more sparsely populated places; all these counties he's doing well in have only a relative few votes in each. One by one they're adding up their small tallies and for Clinton's chances it is, as I describe it at one point in the night, looking like death by a thousand paper cuts.

But we need to be sure that big cities like Columbus or Cleveland won't deliver enough votes to push Clinton ahead. These kinds of urban counties have so many voters they can sometimes change a state all by themselves. In fact, Democrats often rely on them to do just that. Tonight Cleveland is counting more slowly than other places. We assume there are about 650,000 votes, and half of them are still uncounted.

We plug in a most-outrageous-case scenario. Clinton is tracking in Cleveland just under what a typical Democrat, or Obama, got in past years, at 67 percent of what's in so far. So what would happen if she got an astounding 80 percent or even 90 percent? (Which she won't: I test the extremes to be extra sure before making a call like this.) We figure she'd still lose the state. And besides, the turnout there—as in some other Democratic areas—looks laggard compared to other counties.

I give the control room the call, and Ohio lights up Republican red. We move on from Ohio, but we don't forget that pattern we saw, the way it favored Trump. We'll use that later.

•　　•　　•

People always ask me if I get nervous on these nights, but I've learned that anxiety—in this or in anything, maybe—for me comes from not knowing what's coming next. Our whole job is to *know* what's going on, though, and we don't make a call unless we really believe we do. So I try to use nervousness as a test, asking myself if I think I'll be nervous *after* I call this race. What I don't want is for more votes to come in and make me wonder if it had been a smart call or not, looking back once it's done and declared. So far on my watch we've never had to reverse anything. When you take this job you do your best to protect all that network history and reputation with every call, but it's important to have a sense of perspective, too. I have colleagues across this news organization covering war and facing real life-threatening danger around the world. My friends and colleagues stand in combat zones and riots and hurricanes. This is just a storm of statistics.

The first time I ever sat at one of these Decision Desks, I had just been hired at CBS, not too long out of graduate school; it was 2002 and my approach was a little more cautious. My then-boss and mentor, Kathy Frankovic, had plunked me down and assigned me the easy races, expected blowouts, and my suggestions for calls—which is all the weight they carried, just suggestions—would then ladder up to her. There was a governor's race where the incumbent was heavily favored to win, and though he ultimately did, right after poll closing his lead was small. It was my first time trying to find the mix of gumption and calculation that the job demands; even with all the numbers flashing on all those screens, there is no formula for that. I didn't want to look hesitant. But I wanted everyone to know that as the new guy, I understood the metrics, and that I wouldn't make calls just based on what I "thought" would happen. Kathy asked if I was ready to call and I recommended no. I got a quick "okay then," and that was that. I called it a bit later when it made more sense. It turned out no one really cared what time that race got called. She just wanted to see that even under pressure I was thinking it through. That's still very often just the best, simplest test.

Midnight

Hours pass and neither Trump nor Clinton has won much more; things are still too tight. The Upper Midwest is a large bloc of uncalled states, grayed out on the screen, neither lit up red nor blue. Wisconsin is close, as are Michigan, Pennsylvania.

We come back from a commercial break and I do a live segment at the touchscreen, where I game out possible Trump paths to victory from here, state by state—what might happen if we do call each of them for Clinton or Trump. "He has to win Wisconsin?" one of our anchors, Scott Pelley, asks me about Trump's prospects.

"He's got options," I respond, "but it's most likely his path goes through Wisconsin," I say, pointing it out on the state map from among its other unlit neighbors across the Rust Belt.

Minnesota is grayed out, too. Before the night began we had defined the "Battleground" list, the states to watch most closely because they could swing either way. Minnesota wasn't included. It had voted Democratic in every presidential election since 1972 and we'd assumed it would keep on doing so. Over at a producer's desk, they pitch a story to the broadcast control room to do a deep-dive look at its exit polls.

"Minnesota isn't on the Battleground list," the control room says, surprised that it's being flagged for attention.

The producer responds, "That's the point!"

1:00 a.m.

Sometime past 1 a.m. the commentators on set start musing on what a Trump presidency could look like. We haven't called the presidency, but people were reading their own patterns now just by staring at the national map. We haven't called either Maine or New Hampshire, two usually Democratic states we would have put in Clinton's column hours ago had this night been going her way.

I eat another energy bar. Our producer has been kind enough to stash a plastic bag full of them under the desk for me. There was catered food somewhere, but I never left the desk long enough to find it. Murray Edelman's trying to eat salad—I'm not sure where he got it—though he doesn't have a fork, and no one is about to cross the studio or leave the screens to get one.

We divvy up the states among the team. We've called Nevada for Clinton, and Colorado, too. Our decision models on those never really wavered from pointing to wins for her. They were not like the midwestern states—but then, these western states apparently didn't have as many of the kinds of voters who were in flux, late deciders. Nor did they show the same kind of patterns that we were watching in the big eastern cities, where turnout in Democratic strongholds was still running well below 2012's levels. We finally call Maine, too, but these Clinton wins feel like afterthoughts. The presidency still hinges on the Midwest. Bob Schieffer notes that Trump is within range. Trump was 26 electoral votes away. The cameras pan across the map and I hear Scott say ". . . after hours of counting, the votes are so close CBS News has been unable to make a projection." Our cameras cut to the live shot inside the Javits Center, Clinton's gathering, an aerial view of the stage, an empty wood podium. At our anchor desk, Norah O'Donnell reports that Clinton's campaign chair, John Podesta, was headed to that stage to tell the crowd things were too close to call. "Is it too close to call," anchor Gayle King says, "or not wanting to accept reality?"

We all use that phrase "too close to call" a lot on these kinds of nights. At the Desk the language we're thinking in is more nerd-speak: "What we want to know is so small and precise that our measurements can't show it yet." It's something every pollster faces whenever you set out to describe what's going on, though not usually under this kind of time crunch: what kind of error can you live with?

The answer depends on what you need to explain. If we were discussing "favorable" ratings in a regular public opinion poll, no one would parse the difference between a couple of points here and there. But tonight we want to know the winner in what will be a one-point election, so now we need an estimate that's got even less error than that.

2:00 a.m.

The broadcast went live to Trump campaign headquarters, now full of people in red "Make America Great Again" hats as Major Garrett did his stand-up report. Trump was up a point in Pennsylvania, just over seventy thousand votes out of millions cast. Major says that Trump's people felt confident they could win it but were waiting for confirmation from the news organizations. That word, confirmation, caught my ear. Certainty is the bar everyone sets for us.

Murray and Mark Gersh parse Pennsylvania and are working through scenarios, trying to get to that sense of certainty. Mark is hunched with that Alabama cap pulled down and no space between its brim and his spreadsheet. In Wisconsin, I see Milwaukee has only three-quarters of the total votes we expected to be cast there, compared to other counties that are showing turnout closer to the way they typically do. That's a big difference in a tight race. If we'd seen this three hours ago we'd have dismissed it as too unusual, too hard to believe, but tonight we've already seen lower turnout from Democrats in other key places in other key states, the just-not-quite-good-enough support that Clinton's getting.

Seeing consistent patterns elsewhere makes you confident you can fill in the gaps in places that are still unknown. We call Wisconsin for Trump. In the end, when the count was finished, heavily Democratic Milwaukee would cast a lot fewer votes than it did in 2012.

In Pennsylvania, our statistical models still have Trump ahead in the Lehigh Valley, the working-class areas in the eastern part of the state, where coal and manufacturing jobs declined but the new economy hadn't taken root to replace them. It's unusual for a Republican to do so well there, but it, too, is consistent with Trump's campaign and with what we're seeing tonight. These are the sorts of voters he's been winning, and only Philadelphia now stands between Trump and the presidency. We start subtracting, trying to figure if votes in the city will change the direction of the state. But while turnout is *up* statewide in Pennsylvania, turnout in Philadelphia looks *down*. We're trying to find out if they've actually counted everything there, and we might not otherwise believe that turnout pattern, either, except that it's another case of what we've been seeing all night, in an array of places—especially heavily Democratic places—in state after state. The patterns tell a story. We believe what we consistently see, so consistently now that we didn't need to see any more. It was enough to know.

I reach for the intercom one more time and make that call for Trump.

Somewhere in the hours following, everyone left, the lights dimmed. Just after 5 a.m., as dawn approached, I was still hanging around at the Desk. I'd been up twenty-four straight hours now, having done a *CBS This Morning* segment on what was now the previous day. I checked one more time in case any returns had still trickled in from the West Coast, three time zones back, and got ready to leave.

In the coming days I listened to people spurred by the surprises of this night ask about how polling worked, and how we measure things— and whether, in a larger sense, there was something more happening in the country, something they couldn't have made out from a map or a single number. I thought they were right to be asking these questions. And it made the events of this night feel more like the beginning of a story than the end of one.

I crossed the newsroom on my way out and I wandered past the *CBS This Morning* producers as they prepped their morning-after show, just to check if they needed a recap from me, maybe to explain what I'd just seen. At first, with their heads down at their keyboards, they half nodded and said maybe, the show lineup was still coming together. Then they looked up at me, and I could tell they were a little taken aback by what must have been my haggard look and the bags under my eyes. They smiled and very kindly said no, thanks. Go get some sleep.

Chapter Two

Why Didn't You Call Me?

For a lot of things that might seem implausible if we didn't know better, you can at least go watch them work. We see a heavy airliner take flight, even if we can't figure the physics under its wings; we can feel our headache go away with an aspirin even if we flunked out of chemistry. Polling, though, has always had a bit of a problem in this regard. Even if you know that most polls do the job well, the science that drives them still seems to hinge on this odd, counterintuitive notion that we can somehow talk to just a few people and learn about the whole country. It's an idea you can't easily watch in action.

If anything, a lot of our experiences just get in the way. Our friends tell us we're special, which is why they picked us in the first place. The advertisements we see all around us want us to think we're special—or can be for just a few dollars, anyway; we love to get those little greeting cards when our birthday rolls around, telling us we're one of a kind, the best—indeed, unique.

That's a nice idea, but the pollster knows it isn't so.

Now as I say that, please don't think we pollsters haven't got feelings. It's just that we've got to put aside the idea we're all unique, at least for a minute, to get to how polls work.

Instead of greeting cards, most of the comments we get from viewers each time we do a survey say things like "Why didn't you call me?" Or often a more pointed version of it: "You didn't call *me* . . . so your poll can't be right." That can sting a bit—as I said, we do have feelings—but at least I've got good company. Comments like these have been routine since the earliest days of modern polling in the 1920s and 1930s. Back then polling pioneer George Gallup himself noted that the question of "Why wasn't *I* interviewed?" was the top one he'd gotten from the public for most of his career. In one such letter a dismayed reader wrote, "I am 44 years old and have never been polled by you." In her history of polling, *The Averaged American*, Sarah Igo reported another particularly witty note to Gallup: "As I have skeptically been following your recent polls," a reader wrote him, "I have been conducting one of my own. The first question is: do you know of anyone that has ever been polled by Gallup? . . . Well needless to say I again fail to find anyone to say yes." Or this one: "I notice you always say 'The Public' in the headline, but further down in very small print you say the question was put to a carefully selected sample of 1,536 persons. Now how in the world, by any stretch of the imagination, can 1,536 people be termed 'the public'?"

The fact that pollsters today get the same questions that giants of the industry got generations ago makes me feel connected to history, but also uneasy that something fundamental remains unsettled. Pollsters are still not completely or universally persuasive on how all this comes together, even after eighty years of trying. I've seen a lot of pollsters answer these kinds of questions by emphasizing the fact that we *could* have called you, even though we didn't. While that's true from a theoretical, statistical standpoint, it's hardly satisfying on your end; kind of like saying we thought about asking you to the dance but went with someone else instead. A way to think of it is that you've got a lot in common with a lot of people. And we're going to leverage that fact to make sure you get your voice heard.

For the sake of argument, let's say someone back in 2012 decided to vote for Mitt Romney for president. We know there were 60,930,672 other people in the country exactly like that individual in that regard. They all may have come to the idea from different paths, or from similar paths, but that characteristic among them is precisely shared.

Are you over 65 years old? There are about 49 million Americans who share that characteristic with you. A woman? More than 125 million.

Let's say you happen to be a Republican voter today. We can estimate there are about 45 million people in America just like you in that particular way. There are various types of Republicans, of course, so that shared characteristic alone won't be enough for us to understand all that we need to understand about you, but it's a start. You probably have more in common with most of them, at least politically, than you don't.

If we want to get more specific, let's say you're a politically moderate female voter who lives in the Northeast? There are about 6.1 million people who share that with you by my count. You get the idea.

Next consider what we learn from polls. Most polls are measuring opinion as it stands nationwide and the broader brushstrokes of what moves it, so we're out to describe the population, not you in particular. It's why I try to write poll headlines that read "55 percent of *Americans* think . . ." and not poll headlines that say "*You* think."

To the extent polls can ever say something about you in particular, it is through the lens of something you share or don't share with some other portion of the population, however large or small a proportion that may be; which group you belong to, or whether you're like the majority, or like the minority, for instance. And of course there are idiosyncratic or nuanced—and, yes, special—ways that you personally came to whatever ideas you hold. There are things like where you grew up, where you work, what you read, which people and family and events influenced you, and so on, all of which are your stories and your experiences alone.

When I say none of us is special, I'm really talking about the big measures that we're trying to quantify in polls: whether people approve or disapprove of something, will vote or not vote, want to buy or not buy. In those regards, there are indeed things about each of us that are exactly alike in others, enough so that plenty of other people can represent you in a poll, even when you aren't surveyed yourself.

We can widen out the measures of similarity between people a little bit, too. Sometimes folks write in to us after they see a new poll and tell us that no one they know in their town or their book club was called for our poll, just like the people who wrote letters to George Gallup. Fair enough. But yours is not the only town of that type in America. I'm not saying your town is typical, or average on some metric, but merely that it isn't unique on every measure, either. Chances are we did talk to someone from a similar-enough place, and that they represented you.

Whatever side you're on, there's an emotional part to just wanting to be included. Lots of people rightly and simply have a desire to be counted in things that they care about, and that also drives some of these questions about who's included in polls. Back when the industry was newer and people wondered what the use of polls even was, Gallup and the early practitioners argued that the benefits of doing scientific polling offered a way of giving voice to "the people," a voice that they contended was an essential part of a healthy democracy. But as Sarah Igo notes, that idea also—somewhat ironically—invites people to then wonder why they, themselves, weren't asked to weigh in for the poll. After all, democracy means every person gets a vote, so then why shouldn't everyone be included in the poll. Plus, people just like to think that they, themselves, can be determinative in things. So if this poll is going to be held up as the voice of the people, then the idea of you being represented by someone else can certainly rub the wrong way, even aside from the technical feasibility of it all.

That reminds us of the flip side to all this, too, that there are a lot of people who are *not* like you, and who disagree with you, whether or not you happen to know them or hang around with them. They get represented in polls alongside all those folks who do agree with you. We often get folks telling us that "no one I know" or "no one I've talked to" agrees with the majority findings of the poll. Part of the skepticism when we see a poll finding depends, frankly, on whether we like the findings. More and more in a heavily partisan country, partisans tend to look a little more askance at polls that show their point of view might not be as popular as they'd like it to be. And today more than ever, there are plenty of places you go to find a critique of one—or just about anything else for that matter—or just to have your own point of view reinforced, to feel like there's more people on your side than perhaps there truly are. Sometimes when people lament, "You didn't call me," they believe that their view is in fact a lot more prevalent, and that had they somehow been counted, the numbers might have tilted more to their viewpoint.

The people you know and talk to most are probably, on balance, more like you than not, in a lot of ways just by virtue of the fact that you've come to know them, and on a lot of those measures we described. They probably live near you, or work in the same industry, and they may have had some of the same general life experiences. (This is one reason, if we survey you, we wouldn't ask you to then pass the phone to a friend for them to take the survey, too.) But just because your view isn't in the majority at the moment doesn't mean we didn't account for it, or that there is even a small number who share it. If, let's suppose, "only" 40 percent of the country agrees with you, that might not make a headline, but that's still millions and millions of people.

For confirmation one need only look at the large numbers who, whether your side won or lost, *didn't* vote the way you did; or aren't the same age as you; or don't live in the kind of place you do. Forget politics entirely and think of all the people you see using the popular but silly products you would never buy, or who see all those movies that seem to make money even though you've never seen them. We're confronted every day by evidence that there are plenty of people not like us in a lot of ways, too. It's a big country, and you don't need a pollster to tell you that.

In many respects all of this goes to the essence of quantitative social science, the part of science where polling lives. It's a field of study where we make inferences about people and their behavior by observing the patterns of large numbers of them, rather than any particular person, and it depends—in part—on the idea that each of us shares at least something, or can be compared with each other.

So even when we didn't poll you, there were people just like you, at least in the important, overarching themes we're working with, whom we did include. Most are probably numerous enough that they really aren't that hard to find, and—if it makes you feel better—they at least agree with you. They answered the questions the same way you would have, had it been you. It doesn't end there, either. We very well might try you next time, at which point it'll be up to you to represent all those other folks you agree with.

Then once you are included in one of our surveys, representing all those other people like you is a big responsibility, and we depend on you to do it. We really appreciate it when you do. You might not be unique, at least not in your answers—but to us pollsters you will be very special indeed.

The Sample Scoop

If you do take the poll, there won't be a lot of other people in it with you. It often seems puzzling that polling samples are small groups of people, while the population of the country runs into the hundreds of millions. It is perfectly reasonable to wonder why this works. We're only talking to .0004 percent of America, or, on Election Night, we're calling races with just a few dozen precincts out of thousands reporting.

The first step is to forget for a moment anything about the specific size of the poll, be it one thousand people or ten thousand people, and right now simply think in terms of knowledge about the world—knowledge that you can either get or not get.

There are plenty of times people can gauge how well they know something by what portion of all the available information they have. In school, for instance, when tomorrow's history test covers the whole textbook, but you only read half of it, you can correctly gauge that you're in trouble. (I found this out the hard way a few times.) Or if you're buying a new car, and you haven't read the crash test ratings or found out the gas mileage yet, you could justifiably feel uninformed walking into the dealership. Those are problems of completeness: you haven't seen all the information that's out there, and what you *do* know just will not substitute for what you *don't*.

A poll, as traditionally conceived, does not try to fit into those categories of information gathering. There are other occasions, more akin to polling, when we gauge whether we truly know about something by whether or not we've sampled it well; that is, when we think what we've already seen is a good enough *representation* of all that we have not seen.

It's the restaurant you visit twice, not a hundred times, before you decide if it's good.

A classic analogy for the mechanism behind this was mentioned by Gallup in a chapter he wrote in his book *The Pulse of Democracy* called "Building the Miniature Electorate," in which he compared sampling the country to tasting a "bowl of soup." It's a great analogy that's been used by many pollsters since. I'm going to borrow that from him and show you how it works, but I'm going to change the recipe, so to speak, and talk about my grandmother's Bolognese sauce instead. That's what I thought of when I was learning this, and because I'm willing to bet my grandmother's sauce tasted way better than George Gallup's soup.

My grandmother used to stand there all day on Sundays cooking up this sauce. She'd make vats of it no matter how big or small the family gathered around would be, and she never wrote down any recipes, maybe because that kept it special, and probably because this was just one of those watch-and-learn, oral traditions passed down through the family.

Now and again she'd ask us to—or more often, *let* us—taste some as she went. Then she'd ask us how it tasted. (Which, looking back now, I realize she was just being polite, as she would not have changed a thing no matter what I'd said.) But I never answered, "Well, I only had a scoop, I need to eat the whole vat before I can answer." I'd *sampled* to get my information, so I could answer because I knew that what she served me in a spoon or a dish was probably a very good representative sample of *all* the sauce, enough for me to know the thing we cared about learning: the taste.

The sauce had different ingredients in it. There was chopped meat, parsley, sometimes ground sausage; garlic, tomatoes that she'd strained the seeds out of with a funky contraption that looked like fan pressed over a metal mesh. There was some combination of salt and other spices.

Think of all that in the same way you can think of the populace as having different opinions or types of people in it. The underlying mechanism that makes sampling work here is that idea of representation again. The meat I got in my sample bowl was assumed to be enough like *all the other pieces* of meat, including those still in that kitchen pot; same for the pieces of garlic, which were perhaps a little different from each other in shape here and there, but substantially they all tasted about the same *as the ones I didn't get.* The same was even true for each little grain of salt. Each of those pieces of meat or garlic was alike enough to the other pieces of meat and garlic to represent their kind in my bowl, specifically on that item of taste, which was the item we cared about. Here's where that idea of similarity on the individual level comes together to help us put together a smaller, but representative, sample of all those parts.

When you judge a poll, don't judge it by what portion of the whole it is any more than you would expect to eat five gallons of Bolognese sauce to judge it because you "only" tasted a scoop. As pollsters or as anyone trying to use a sample, the test for us in these situations is not a question of what size *portion* of the whole we have, it's a question of how *like the whole* our portion is. We ask ourselves: does what we've seen or experienced contain all the essential elements of the whole?

So think of a good polling sample as a microcosm of the country, where what you have in front of you has the power to teach you about everything you don't see. Judge the success of a sample not by what percentage of the country you cover, but by how like the country it is, in miniature.

Now here's the other fun part. Notice that your sauce sample can tell you what you want to know—the taste—no matter how big the vat in the kitchen that it is drawn from is. You can get this idea of the taste just as well from your one decent-size scoop, whether my grandmother had made ten gallons of sauce back there, or a hundred gallons of it. Likeness is likeness, and you can learn from it, no matter how many other alike items are out there.

My grandma never actually checked to make sure everyone had gotten all the right ingredients in their dish. She'd just reach in and ladle it out and odds were you would get all the pieces in proportion, the same for everyone, and we didn't need to sit there and specify three pieces of sausage, please. It seemed to work out, or at least no one ever got something different enough to complain. All she was doing was being fair to her guests, but it turns out there was a certain sampling power in her approach, too, because it meant she was letting what was in the pot come through. If the sauce had three pieces of garlic or six chunks of sausage per cubic inch, that's what would invariably show up in your bowl. In the Bolognese sauce it was easy to know, of course, that you'd gotten all the ingredients. In a national poll, we want to make sure the sample has the same proportions as the U.S. Census on things like age (talking to the old and the young and everyone in between), region (north, south, east, and west), education, and race, so that all those groups can be represented, so that the composition is itself representative. Think of these like the ingredients in the recipe we try to re-create in bowl after bowl. That's the idea, and frankly, it's the ideal. Out in the world, away from the comfort of grandma's kitchen, things will get trickier. There is no national ladle. We'll need to go out and find people.

Meanwhile, think of a good sample as a microcosm, where each piece you get in it is alike enough to those you don't get in it that you can let those pieces speak for the whole. We can try to create this nation-in-miniature because each of us shares at least some fundamental and measurable things with a lot of other people who get selected when we don't.

I like to think that's more than just a practical notion for polling.

You're connected to a lot of people, which is a good thing. They can stand up for you: say what you'd say; think how you think. We can use representativeness to learn something about the world when we cannot see it all.

And there's power for us all in that idea.

Chapter Three

Finding You

Let me take you to a place quite deliberately far away from the lights and cameras of any television studio. It's a cheerfully conventional, fluorescently lit office space nestled in a perfectly pleasant office park just off Route 78 in Allentown, Pennsylvania.

"Hello, my name is —— and I am calling on behalf of CBS News with a poll on current events."

That's the exact start of what an interviewer says when someone picks up their phone and it's us, the CBS News poll, on the line. Dozens of professional interviewers in rows of cubicles are on the phones here at the SSRS, Inc. call center, wearing hands-free headsets and sitting before computer screens that flash the poll questions one by one. In the hours leading up to this, around conference tables in their meeting rooms, they've already read through those questions and practiced saying them aloud. Standing amid them and listening now as the poll is under way, it's the sound that strikes you more than the visuals—but then, that's kind of the point, this chorus of questions. When it works, the tone is a deft reading of scripted lines, delivered with the friendliness and flow that suggests a conversation, but a touch too much we-have-business-to-do pace to really become one.

"We're not selling anything," an interviewer can offer if a potential respondent sounds skeptical, which many rightly are in this age of telemarketers and solicitors. "Just doing an opinion poll on interesting subjects for research purposes."

Seventy percent of these calls are to cell phones, because that's what Americans use more of now—many, exclusively—so good phone polling has gone where Americans are, as it should. (I'll repeat that because a lot of people still think we don't call cell phones. We mostly call cell phones.) When it is a cell, interviewers first ask if the respondent is doing anything else that requires their full attention, and if they are, we'll call back later. If it is a landline ringing in the living room of a home somewhere out there in America, anywhere from Anchorage, Alaska, to Alligator Point, Florida, then every interviewer is trained to cheerfully stick to the science: respondents have to be from among the people in the household, and we'll happily explain why if asked. If we're dialing random phone numbers out into the world, we don't know who is at the other end of the line, or how many people live in the house. The computer generates a random pick onto the interviewer's screen, asking for the oldest or youngest, man or woman, and we ask to speak to whoever fits that bill, if there is such a person, so long as they're over eighteen. "This is a scientific study," interviewers can explain if the person on the line asks, What about me? "We need to make sure that all households and all the adults who live in those households have a fair chance of being randomly selected to participate."

The caller will make arrangements to call back someone who is selected but not at home; that way we try to reduce the chances of just interviewing people who happened to be home when we called. Eventually we catch up with a lot of people, though many we just never do. Larger-scale studies that have longer time frames might keep trying over weeks, but ours typically make a few calls over a couple of days.

And then off we go.

Often the first question is: "Do you approve or disapprove of the way (whoever is president) is handling his job as president?"

It will take three or four days on average, hundreds of interviewers calling number after number, to finish this poll. Make no mistake, this has gotten a lot harder to do. You're just not that easy to find on the phone anymore. In a typical poll these interviewers will try over 25,000 phone numbers to get around 1,000 people to complete the survey. Twenty years ago that ratio was dramatically smaller, just a few thousand to get 1,000 completes.

We know that a sample can reflect the country. Making it work in practice is a challenge—and probably the first challenge for any pollster. In theory, everyone is findable, and, in theory, each time we draw a person into our theoretical sample they just go right in, no one refuses, everyone is willing and waiting at home to be surveyed.

In real life, that's hardly the case. And the burden of finding people is entirely on the pollster, not them: the pollster has to be the one asking them to join the poll, not the other way around. If we just let anyone or everyone call us, we'd ultimately get a collection tilted toward the most passionate or rabid partisans who are looking to vent or influence things, like trying to learn what percentage of all Americans are baseball fans by posting a sign-up sheet outside Yankee Stadium.

I certainly hadn't thought about places like this phone room when I got interested in politics. I had gotten my PhD and studied voting with a quantitative bent, trying to learn how the political world worked by measuring it and numbering and decoding it all. Political scientists like me are trained to use polling data as one (of many) tools for doing that. In fact, the poll questionnaire is literally called an "instrument," as in a measuring instrument, the way I suppose an astronomer might think of a telescope, though their goal is to learn about the stars. So you quickly learn that before you can get to the fancy maps and breaking news, you need to have the right instrument to properly see what you want to see in the first place. In our case, we want to learn about people, and first you have to find them.

In earlier days of political polling in the 1940s, selecting people had meant going door-to-door, asking to interview them in person. By the late 1960s and early 1970s, enough Americans had phones that pollsters could call instead, and the poll results could start to deliver something reasonably close to that microcosm of America—though there was plenty of debate about that among pollsters initially. It might seem odd from today's perspective where so much has been done by phone for so many years, but whenever a new approach has come along it has to prove itself, and polling by phone was no different.

Nor was it easy, or fast. The phone system wasn't made for pollsters, it was made for phone companies, and pollsters were simply coming along and trying to take advantage of it. It's best to think of the phone system as a platform for possibly finding people, and it can be handled well, or not.

What the early phone polls often found was tedium. All those digits that make up a phone number mean millions and millions of possible combinations of numbers, and not all of them had a real house and phone attached to them. Many sat unused. There were so many of those that pollsters really couldn't just make up a number, call it, and expect to find someone sitting at home waiting to respond. So calling was expensive to pay for the interviewers who were dialing away and coming up empty. Taking numbers from the white pages (the phone book, a massive listing of names and numbers that few under age thirty might recognize today) risked missing unlisted numbers, the people who'd declined to be included in the phone book.

A big innovation that helped make it all work had actually come at CBS News. Warren Mitofsky, then heading elections and polling for the network, wasn't just a statistician but also a savvy dealmaker. He convinced the phone company to sell him its private files of all the area codes and prefixes—those digits before the dash on your phone number—to which they'd actually assigned groups of real people. Along with his former colleague from the Census Joe Waksberg, they showed how randomly dialing using those would produce a quality sample. Even today, an interviewer working at one of those calling stations would see numbers pop up that are often still influenced by those ideas, with area codes and subregions selected and then a random set of digits tacked on, hence the term for it, random digit dialing.

As a result, phone polling got faster and a lot less expensive as it got easier to find a working number. Speed was exactly what a news network demanded: Mitofsky started the CBS News/*New York Times* poll in 1975. The polling they began was transformative then, and it's still meaningful now for trends and for context. I can look through polls from that time like they're the crosstab equivalents of Polaroid Instamatic photos of a bygone era. There are Americans wary of the Soviet Union, or wondering about an unknown named Jimmy Carter. "There also seems to be an increase in the number of couples living together without being married," from 1977. "Do you think this is okay, or is it something that's always wrong, or doesn't it matter much to you?" (48 percent: "Always wrong.") The numbers and findings go on through the decades from there, all loaded into digital files now, but still some copies remain on faded typewritten memos and handbooks of campaigns long gone, black notebooks with punched-hole pages that threaten to fall away from the three silver rings inside as you crack one open, questionnaires with answers hand-circled in pencil from the days before interviewers used computers to record answers. "Do you approve or disapprove of the way Ronald Reagan is handling foreign policy?" (Circled: "2: No.")

With more polling demand from the news, Mitofsky hired the young political scientist Kathy Frankovic, who'd been teaching at the University of Vermont and came down to work for what she thought would be a short stint on an exciting new venture in New York. Kathy stayed at CBS for decades and became one of the nation's great pollsters in her own right, eventually taking over for Mitofsky when he left to start his own company. And my own life changed when, nearly thirty years after that, in 2002, Kathy was looking for a young political scientist to work for her. That's when I found myself sitting at a Mexican restaurant in Orange County, California, where she'd flown in for a few hours just to talk to me about a job.

I was not in the news business and, much like Kathy all those years earlier, it had not been my goal to join it, though I loved the idea of its fast pace and relevancy. I'd recently finished my doctorate, and I had some technical skills usable for polling, too, but had Kathy not hired me I might have become a professor or a private pollster. I did have one interaction with the media when, in 2001, the year before I met her, I had helped out *USA Today* in a post-election study of what happened in the Florida 2000 contest. I like to think it signaled to Kathy that I could work with newspeople and put things into explainable form in fairly short order.

We talked a lot about politics that day, the way the George W. Bush administration had handled 9/11, the way the public had reacted. Kathy told me about what she'd learned doing polls on all that. I noted that word: here was one of the foremost practitioners in the field talking about what she was still *learning* as much as what she knew. I still carry that lesson. A good survey asks questions you don't know the answer to. Actually, it turned out to not be very subtle with Kathy, either. In the years that followed whenever something didn't quite work out as we planned, or when something surprised us, she would exclaim: "Well, we learned something!"

Kathy later told me she'd been looking for a political scientist, because the survey and election business for the news meant not knowing what you'd need to figure out next. You might be rooting around for old vote data from some county somewhere for a surprisingly competitive race one day, or polling on a brand-new topic the next. That just made it sound more exciting. We talked about whether I would actually leave Southern California, not an unreasonable question when one is sitting on a patio eating enchiladas in the sunshine. In fact, I thought silently, I'd always sworn to myself I wouldn't. For reasons of both food and sunshine, specifically. Then again, this was a rare chance to measure history up close and to learn from the best in the business. I took the job.

"Have I Reached You at Home?"

When I arrived at CBS, the phone dialing center was far smaller—it could be, because it was easier to find people without dialing as many numbers as today—and at the time it was also located in the building right across the street from my new office in the Broadcast Center. The phone room there is long gone, but the musty smell of the hallway that led to it, which I pass by now and again to park my bike in the garage, still reminds me of that mix of anxiety and excitement you get in the first days on a new job.

That time was exciting for someone with an interest in crunching the numbers of politics, and it was also a little tough, having come after a quick cross-country move. I'd gotten married that year and though my wife, Lina, and I both hoped to stay in California, we agreed I should go on ahead to New York for an opportunity that might never come around again. We'd met in graduate school, and she was tied down for a bit longer to a university teaching job, but luckily she landed a job as a professor in New York. Today when work has such long hours sometimes we joke I might as well be across the country.

I'd been trained to put things into formulas. Now, over at that phone room, I'd listen in on interviewers some nights, which pollsters routinely do to get a sense of how the questions are going over. I could hear how regular Americans responded; hear the human side of it. Some paused long and hard, giving thought to each, the calls dragging on as they did—but it also dispelled for me the notion that a lot of people just spit out any old answers top of mind. It was mostly quiet, and distractions, when they came, were on the order of dinner dishes clanking or televisions blaring, but you could usually tell people were trying to focus, asking to repeat a question, blurting out an answer with conviction as soon as they heard the choice they wanted, which always drew a polite continuation from the interviewer, who had to read every word to everyone.

Some folks did grow impatient ("How much longer will this take?"), which still sits with me whenever we are writing a questionnaire that goes on for a while. It was during the time in the run-up and at the start of the Iraq War in 2002 and 2003, and tensions then, as now, were a mixture of the fear of terrorism and the sadness of 9/11 and the unease about where the U.S. was headed next. You could hear that in a lot of the answers and the voices, and in comments dropped in as asides, unrecorded, the touch of ambiguity in between the categorized boxes of the answers.

The people on the other end of this line were a diverse group, as they ought to be, but the sample leaned toward older people; they're just at home more. To this day, older Americans are still much easier to reach. Some plainly had time on their hands, especially then, when questionnaires could easily run a tedious thirty minutes. Today polls are a lot shorter, on the phone about fifteen minutes or less, and quicker online, taking five minutes or so. You've got to accommodate people's busy lives. It clearly helps to have the poll coming from a major media outlet. We do not pay money to phone respondents as incentive to take it, but if people do want to have their voices added, they know the poll will get attention and be national in scope. Plus, politics seems to have a way of getting people to talk, and of making even the casually interested willing to take time for something with an air of importance.

Time apparently has grown scarcer. In the decades that had followed the start of the CBS News poll, more Americans were working longer hours, and fewer and fewer were at home to answer the phone. Prosperity meant some could go out more for leisure when they weren't working. Time got a little more precious for everyone when they were home, too, so that people had to carefully consider the minutes they'd spend doing the interview. In the 1990s, dial-up modems with their buzzing and ping-ing connections to the early Internet meant interminable busy signals for a pollster trying to get through, as did the middle-class teenagers not eligible for surveys hogging the phone lines. Telemarketers seemed to make more people suspicious of just who it was behind that ringing, when it did ring, so answering machines and caller ID devices let people screen their calls. Polling rooms like CBS's had to make sure it said "CBS News" on the caller ID, and interviewers actually did record messages on answering machines that they'd be calling back another time.

What pollsters call the "response rate" began to drop—that's the por-tion of people who could have been included in the poll that actually do get included. Even in the late 1990s overall response rates for major polls were reportedly still up in the mid-30-percent range, which isn't bad. Then, more than four out of ten households with eligible adults in them cooperated, that is, they agreed to take the survey when they did answer—all of which was still okay considering all the factors that could lead polls to miss someone, or all the good reasons why someone might refuse. When we consider how many people reflexively say "I wouldn't have time" or "I wouldn't want to talk" to a pollster, that was evidence that in fact there were plenty of people who really did want their voices heard. By 2012, response rates had dipped to under 10 percent, where they remain today. And the cooperation rate, with many people now saying no to us, had also dipped; so not only were people harder to find, but they simply declined more often when found.

There are few things that make phone pollsters more nervous than these statistics. The good news so far—even if it feels counterintuitive—is that the few people who do still take the polls aren't that entirely different from the ones who don't, at least on the demographics we can measure, and the national presidential polls done by phone in 2016 were very close to the final results, even better than they'd been in 2012.

Lately we wondered just who it was that said no to taking the poll, even after—or especially after—hearing who it was doing the poll. So I saved the phone numbers we'd randomly dialed in 2016 from a few surveys, including from all the people who had said no and hung up. We didn't know anything else about them besides that phone number, which we'd randomly dialed. So we looked up those numbers after the fact and compared them to the voter lists, to see what kinds of households they belonged to. We couldn't find them all, but the numbers we were able to find were more likely to have household profiles with independents or Democrats. Their demographics were the kind who are just plain harder to reach anyway, younger, often lower-income, and tight on time.

Plenty worry it's all just a matter of years before this way of interviewing becomes undoable. It'll probably just get even more expensive instead, or take an increasingly careful pollster to do right. But the fewer people who answer the phone, or don't have time to take the poll, the more potential there is that all the people we find will be unlike those we don't.

When we see that happening, when a poll doesn't get people in the right proportions as the Census (or whatever the characteristics of the place we're sampling), the demographic mix like the percentage of men, of women, of younger and older people can get adjusted to match the right ones in a process called weighting. That means some of the people in the poll have to carry a bigger load now, and pick up more of the slack for everyone like them who was left out. (So, suppose your poll gets half as many young people as there actually are in the population. Then each of those young people in your poll might have to carry twice the weight, to balance things out.) Anytime you aren't finding enough people, that adds potential for what we call bias—not "bias" the way people use it in political arguments, like slanted to one argument or another, but in the statistical sense, to mean a systematic error, a poll routinely missing one particular kind of person, unintentionally but often. That's simply the worst thing that can happen to any survey. Especially if you don't know you've missed something. If your poll has a bias and you know it, you can try to correct it. If you can't see it, it stands a real chance to go wrong.

A lot of polls go more directly to voters to try getting around some of the response issues. Instead of randomly generating phone numbers, we tried picking people to call from lists of registered voters. Back in the mid-'00s Kathy threw me right into experimenting for ourselves with this technique, which was increasingly being used by campaigns. I'm telling you about this because while we might use it occasionally today, it really affects how much contact you get from campaign pollsters. States keep those voter lists—that's how they know who's eligible to vote or not—and many of them are publicly available or augmented and maintained by private firms. Pollsters can select people off that list to call, which is known as Registration-Based Sampling. Campaigns make regular use of it to find the people most liable to vote. If you're looking for voters, it's less efficient to call numbers that aren't on the voter list. If you, yourself, are a habitual voter, one who turns out every year and in local races and primaries, it's quite likely you are on someone's list. That's probably the reason you get more calls; or get mail from campaigns; or get more knocks on your door, than your neighbor who hardly ever votes. I'll bet if you are a regular primary voter in New Hampshire, you're less likely to be one of those people asking that question "Why didn't you call me?"

By the mid-'00s some wondered if cell phones might force the end of phone polling altogether. Ironically, they may have ended up saving it.

Early on, cells were expensive for us to call, and for people to get called on, but we dialed them anyway. We dutifully logged what happened when we reached these cell numbers, and it seemed most of our colleagues in the industry were doing the same. When I went and presented at the pollster conferences, the big industry gatherings that fill a hotel with scores of statisticians, I might have expected to find endless discussions on how people felt about government or wars amid the sea of khaki pants and blue blazers and name tags. Instead the conferences were dominated by a long list of panels and endless PowerPoints by researchers trying to gauge which Americans used cells, how often, and how to find them. For regular people in the mid-'00s, calling plans had limited minutes, and especially before smartphones, people didn't leave their cell phones on all the time. There were not many respondents willing to pay or burn those precious minutes to talk to a pollster. Eventually, though, people's cell plans got cheaper, more minutes became free, and the cell phone became the only way to reach so many people that there was simply no other choice but to dial them.

The fact that today most of our respondents take polls on their cell phones has driven up the costs and time required for doing phone polling. A person on a cell phone, even if you get through to them, is more likely to be out doing something where they can't sit and talk to you, even if they want to. It just takes more interviewers more numbers to dial to find the same number of respondents as it did years ago.

Half the nation's households are cell phone only—they have no landline at all. So cell phones are simply the only way to find many people, including groups that are just harder to track down anyway: lower-income Americans—who often work long hours or for whom setting up a landline service can be expensive compared to a cell plan—and younger people, who might be out anywhere doing all sorts of things, as they should be in their twenties. Interestingly, though, once cells are included, the demographics of the overall poll still don't appear to be wildly off from what they used to be before them. Although those low response rates effectively mean not everyone has a realistic chance to get into the poll, so far, the profiles of those who do take them actually haven't changed all that much over recent years.

But, given the prevalence of cell phones, you ought to take a skeptical look at any phone poll that still doesn't call them, and doesn't have at least some sound method of replacing and representing their owners in the sample.

Connecting with You

As Internet use boomed in the mid-'00s, online interviewing was alluring—fast, private, many things news polling wants to be. But sampling from the Internet for a national poll was a challenge. Unlike phone numbers, there was no equivalent single identifier for an individual on the Internet, except maybe for email, and email isn't at all like phone numbers. A pollster can't just make up a name and email address, send, and find somebody. There are just too many possibilities.

For the presidential debates in 2004 we wanted to get instant reaction while John Kerry and George W. Bush were sparring, and the

Internet did seem the fastest way to do that. We set up hundreds of viewers who could sit at home watching and could give feedback as the debate unfolded, moving meters from "dislike" to "like" as the candidates talked. This panel of people had been recruited beforehand by a company called Knowledge Networks, which picked and maintained a representative sample of Americans, and gave Internet service to those who didn't already have it. (It was fun, though I learned then and in subsequent debates that things tend to look fairly predictable: Democrats like what the Democrats are saying, Republicans like what the Republicans are saying, and mostly people respond when the candidates talk about personal feelings.)

Around that same time I met Doug Rivers, the Stanford professor and entrepreneur who joined the CBS Decision Desk to help us call races. Online polling was growing. A lot of businesses were using it. For the media, though, the question was still how to make an online sample look like that ideal microcosm of America we were all after.

Now let me take you out to the other side of the country, just south of Market Street in San Francisco, where the building facades are still those of heavy industry and warehouses, but inside are tech companies. In one of those spaces with soaring ceilings and an open floor plan, the people sitting at computers are in the polling business but they aren't calling anyone. Instead they're managing millions of Americans who take surveys online; sending out invitations to take the poll; processing the data as it comes back.

These survey invitations might start like this, popping up on your screen: "Welcome to YouGov America's Monthly Tracker for CBS News. This is a survey about the President and current events. There are no wrong answers—just your opinions, and we want to hear them. Your answers will be kept completely confidential. If you don't want to answer a question, just skip it and click the next arrow to get to the next page."

By the mid-'00s, Rivers had started the company that would become

YouGov America and amassed a collection of more than one million people, panelists who had agreed in principle to be surveyed online from time to time, usually by clicking onto ads or by taking a first survey. But as alluring as those eye-popping figures seemed as they headed into the millions, that still wasn't good enough. No matter how large the group is, the test for any sample is whether it looks like a microcosm of the country.

We all knew polls also need to be careful not to let volunteers jump into a survey by themselves, and this was another often misused and dangerous practice in the easy, just-click-here online world. Volunteers don't naturally organize themselves into that microcosm of the country; no one refuses a poll saying, "Oh, you already have fifty percent men, and I'm a guy? Well, I don't want to throw off your sample, so I guess I'll keep my views to myself." As with any good pollster, Rivers had to be the one doing the selecting. The challenge was figuring out how to draw a representative sample out of this promising panel to look like one that would have been plucked out of a hopper of all Americans, were such a thing possible.

One approach could have been to pick them one by one based on who they were, selecting men and then women in balance, selecting young and then old until the pollster hit the right proportions, and there certainly were enough to choose from. But pollsters had been down that road before, rather literally, and knew it could cause trouble, at least in their ability to gauge election results in advance; a lesson from the shoe-leather age of polling that served as a warning for the modern one. In the 1940s interviewers for polls had fanned out across towns and cities going door-to-door and neighborhood-to-neighborhood to find participants. They'd had quotas for how many of each kind of person to include, with the types defined in advance—get so many old, so many young, and so on. At the time it had made sense.

But if an interviewer was given a quota to fill of, let's say, women, they could potentially walk into a nice, clean apartment building in a nice neighborhood and fill up their quota of women from there, and not go into the more run-down buildings in low-income neighborhoods to get the poorer women there. Their collection would look like they got "enough" women, but they'd be biasing the sample toward only including wealthier women; just as bad statistically, it wasn't fair to everyone, if the women were selected just because they were living in a spot convenient for the interviewer. Then if wealthy women they included voted differently from poor women they didn't include, the polls could go wrong.

In 1948, partly because of these kinds of selection methods, things did go wrong. Pre-election polls had the Republican Thomas Dewey leading President Harry Truman by a wide margin, so much so that a Chicago newspaper went to press saying Dewey had won. Once the actual votes were counted and Truman had prevailed, a photo of him gleefully holding up a paper that said "Dewey Defeats Truman" on Election Night became legendary, and nowhere more than in polling circles.

So now if Internet polls selected people this same way, they could suffer the same fate. It was possible to extend the categories of selection down into more fine-grained combinations—for instance, get rich and poor women; get rich older women and poor younger women, and so on. But you might end up stuck with no one who fit your criteria perfectly, or having to make so many deliberate inclusions and exclusions, or judgments about who you wanted beforehand, that you'd need to be a mystic instead of a pollster to guess all the categories right.

Enter big data and faster computers. Rivers knew that there was a wealth of individuals' data sitting, anonymously, in public Census survey files. Here was the U.S. landscape of people from massive Census surveys in all sorts of permutations and combinations, the rich old white males and the rich young white males and the poor old white males and so on. Add to that all the data from voter registration files that was sitting separately on voter records—which themselves were getting a bit better with improved technology—and it was a world of real category combinations just waiting to tell its story. Rivers realized that he could sample that without having to make all those a priori judgments about whom to select, so he did, but with no intention of actually interviewing anyone. There were no names on the file to ask for, anyway. He just wanted to see what a sample of all these anonymous people would look like, across all those variables: age, race, or political affiliation, voting habits, and so on.

Then he turned back to his own panel, whose names he did know, and whom he could interview. He developed a computer model to define a sample of those panelists that, taken as a whole, looked like the sample he'd drawn from the Census files. The key step—which could only be pulled off efficiently with modern computers that could run though the millions of possible combinations involved—was that he didn't select his people one by one on categories like those interviewers who'd gone door-to-door filling a quota. His algorithm was essentially considering everyone possible, on all their important characteristics, trying out per-mutation after permutation of combinations of age, race, sex, and other characteristics. It took into account the fact that even people who had slight differences on one or two items were in fact very similar across many others, and the mass of data available on people opened up that insight. The result came back with the one sample that, considered in its entirety, matched most closely to what target sample from the Census files had looked like. And those folks got the survey.

It was working, and in 2006 the scholarly community took notice as Rivers, along with Steve Ansolabehere, who's also on the Decision Desk, and a host of other top political scientists fielded a large study using the method across U.S. congressional districts that they showed performed better than phone samples, one that they've continued since.

• • •

In 2008 I was tasked with testing this out for ourselves after Doug and Kathy arranged the setup, so here again was another chance for CBS News to explore an emerging technique. I wanted to take the results of the regular CBS News national poll and, as it moved back and forth between Barack Obama and John McCain, look at the data that Doug was collecting state by state at the same time. We combined the two, to explain which battleground states like Ohio, Florida, or North Carolina might be expected to flip as the national numbers moved. We were able to offer a pre-election estimate of the Electoral College and all the states, too, and it worked well.

Rivers and his colleague Delia Bailey wrote a paper assessing their approach and argued that "2008 was the year that Internet polling came of age. . . . Several large academic projects, including the American National Election Study (ANES) . . . and the Cooperative Campaign Analysis Project (CCAP) all collected data using the Internet."

For us, this was increasingly looking like a good way to find voters. By the time the 2012 campaign rolled around, I had become elections director and Doug and I tried a series of estimates of our own in all fifty states, where we simulated an Electoral College outcome for the Obama-Romney race. Our September estimate was spot-on, and our October models were very close to hitting every state the way it finally turned out. It didn't get a lot of attention, frankly, because there were a lot of polling estimates out there competing for eyeballs, most showing much the same thing. But for us the main thing was the test. To me, it was clear this worked and was as good a way to talk to voters as we had available.

Then in 2014 we launched the Battleground Tracker project working along with *The New York Times*, and that had a larger impact, as we reported the estimates across a string of Senate races, along with a congressional seat estimate. It once again performed about the way the phone polls had that year, and in some places a little better. We showed the Republican takeover of the Senate but underestimated the extent of their gains, as many other polls had as well.

In 2016 alone we did more than a hundred surveys this way for both the general election and the primaries, with a speed and volume unmatched in the history of CBS News, and the following year continued with large surveys to follow views of the new president. Access to the Internet had become much less of an issue, certainly at least for politics and voters. By 2017, 88 percent of Americans reported using the Internet and 73 percent had broadband at home. Seventy-seven percent had a smartphone, up dramatically from just 35 percent in 2011. And in a funny way cell phones make this possible, too—or smartphones, specifically—because you can take a poll or survey on your iPhone or Android touchscreen much like you can on your desktop.

Online panels are different from phone polls in a few other respects. Phones call people out of the blue, but panelists online sign up, and companies want them to stay as panel members. So they usually have incentives to offer, such as earning points like in frequent flier programs. This can make it easier to keep and survey groups that polling generally has a hard time finding, and managing who's on a panel is a major task for many of the online polling companies. It's a balance, though. One can wonder if this turns people into professional poll takers, a fair concern countered in turn by the fact that large enough online polling operations don't need to send the same kinds of polls to the same people all the time, and the opinions of those who do regularly take surveys may nonetheless be—and usually are—the same as everyone else's.

You might ask if that brings in respondents who rush through surveys or don't answer carefully, though this can happen on the phone, too. My experience is that people's answers do make sense across a series of questions—they show consistency, which is a time-honored test for whether people are expressing their true views as opposed to just picking responses willy-nilly. And because computers know how much time respondents spend on a digital questionnaire, in ours, at least, we see that most respondents are taking their time.

A panel study, where people are interviewed again and again, is very good at measuring how people's opinions change—or don't—because you can compare their old answers to their new ones. You just have to be careful not to interview them too often, certainly not every day. We used this to good effect on our Nation Tracker surveys where we could show that President Trump's strongest backers stayed reliably firm through the first year of his presidency even as other would-be supporters told us they had drifted away. The panel made it easier to see that it was real people changing their minds rather than our wondering if it was sampling differences.

In the ensuing years a number of other media organizations have started going online, too, with firms like SurveyMonkey and Morning Consult that leverage large numbers of survey participants weighted to represent the country. As online has exploded, I tell people not to think of polls in terms of comparing online panels versus phone surveys as an either-or proposition, just based on the way the interview is conducted. Rather, think of them as different approaches to forming that "nation in miniature." I see the design of the sample as more important than the way the interview is done. In either case there are a lot of decisions to be made about the approach, whom to talk to, how to weight; the poll numbers are increasingly a function of how careful the pollster was.

I also see some important commonalities: both forms have their relatively hardest time getting younger people and minorities to take the survey, and tend to have more older respondents before any adjustments to correct the sample. One might think that online would be filled with millennials who are always attached to their phones, but that's not the case, in fact the opposite. The reality is that deciding to take a survey still appears to be affected by how much time people have, and young people just have a lot of things on their mind other than politics and policy issues. Interest develops along with age.

People today are also more immune to that old pollster's appeal to make "your voice heard" by taking a poll. There are a lot of outlets for expressing your view now; even if they aren't scientific, they can feel more instantaneous. I was in a college classroom not long ago guest-speaking on how polls are done, and one young student raised his hand with what was as much a statement as a question. He held up his smartphone. "If I have an opinion, I can post it anywhere," he said. "I can put it on my Facebook page, I can tweet it, I can rate my professor. Why would anyone need to take your poll to 'make their voice heard' today?"

I tried to make the case that anyone in our CBS polls would be part of a scientific survey, and that the findings would have voice beyond just his circle of followers or friends. He seemed only somewhat persuaded. Part of the answer for us pollsters is to make the surveys and the subjects interesting enough that they engage people. My own sense, empirically and anecdotally, is that most people like being asked something thoughtful.

On our end, pollsters argue a lot, and will undoubtedly keep doing so, over the details of things I've described here. We're scientists by training, and somewhat obsessive and particular about our tools. Sometimes this comes across in op-eds and interviews as pollsters openly wonder about the future of polling. But the best pollsters look for evidence, and the clear evidence we have through our relatively short but successful history is that good pollsters—like some of the ones that I've been lucky enough to come across—keep finding new ways to make things work. And they will keep doing so. It's true that things may not always be done the same way they've always been done, and like any science, the tools will change and evolve. Like any other pursuit, the best practitioners are out inventing its future.

Good pollsters are driven not just by sampling statistics but by the desire to find and talk to people, wherever they are and whatever their habits are. It's up to us pollsters to adjust to them as we always have. Being accurate is our responsibility, but listening to people is our mission.

And okay, I just can't resist the pun here to say it's also our . . . calling.

Chapter Four

How to Avoid Surprises

The **"Reluctant Republicans,"** at first glance, tell a story about why pre-election polls might have gotten the numbers they did in 2016. They're really a big reminder to watch any campaign—and read a poll—like a campaign might.

"Reluctant Republicans" was the label we'd given throughout the fall of 2016 to Republicans unwilling to back their party's nominee, Donald Trump. (John Dickerson and I had followed them through the campaign on *Face the Nation*, I can't recall if it was John or I who came up with the term, but it's nicely alliterative so it was probably John.) Either way, there were plenty of Reluctant Republicans. Some had voted in the bruising primary contests for other Republicans, like Governor John Kasich or Senator Ted Cruz, and weren't ready to switch their allegiance over to Trump; others hadn't partaken in the primaries but simply weren't comfortable with Trump personally. These Reluctant Republicans were about 10 percent or so of their party, in many of the competitive states that we polled. That might not sound like a lot but if you followed the pre-election polls (or at least ours) you knew that they were very impactful, and they were a big part of the reason many state polls showed Trump trailing through October.

Hillary Clinton was getting almost all the Democrats in the polls saying they'd support her, around 90 percent. Meanwhile, these Republican holdouts meant that Trump was lagging sometimes in the high-70s- or low-80s-percent range with people in his own party. These days, that's not good enough, because in our hyper-partisan elections both Republican and Democratic presidential candidates—whoever they are—typically need about 90 percent or more of their party's voters to have a chance to win. There just aren't enough crossover voters for a winning formula to work otherwise.

In our pre-election interviews almost all of these Reluctant Republicans said they would surely have voted for *any* GOP nominee had it been someone *other* than Trump. They did, however, overwhelmingly agree with the idea of changing Washington, and they were in no mood to consider Hillary Clinton instead of Trump. They called themselves moderate or somewhat conservative ideologically and many said they wouldn't vote at all that year, even though they usually had in the past.

Not only were these Republicans holding out, one could tell a plausible story about why they'd never return. Trump was not a conventional candidate to say the least (and voters described him as different from a traditional Republican, which was part of his appeal to many). Trump had been through a competitive primary season, including one in which some in the party had openly talked about ways to take the nomination to the floor of the convention or wrest it from him. The late spring had not seen the usual coalescing of the partisans around their nominee, where all the other candidates and their backers usually fall in line for the sake of party unity. There was even a Never Trump movement, such as it was, with an attendant Twitter hashtag. When the delegates at the Republican National Convention booed Ted Cruz as he didn't endorse Trump, it reminded people that the party was slow to come together. So in the fall if there were 10 percent or so of Republicans who were not with him, it could easily be explained, given that context.

But it was also clear in the fall that this could be viewed as a potential market segment for Trump that wasn't being realized. We noted it in our own poll coverage and on *Face the Nation*. Reince Priebus, Republican National Committee chair at the time, acknowledged on *Face the Nation* that there was a deficit within his party and talked about how the race could and would get back to even if Republicans all came home and backed Trump.

Then came Election Day, and these Reluctant Republicans put their reluctance aside. By a ratio of about four to one, when we reinterviewed them in post-election surveys days after it, these voters reported having voted for Trump after all. Only a quarter of them had actually stayed home, as some had suggested they'd do before the election. Half of them said they'd made their decision in the closing days of the campaign.

We'd seen evidence of this on Election Night, not only geographically in Trump's strong performance across the conservative counties, but in the overall levels of party support that Trump ended up with in the exit polls. Trump did eleven points better among Republicans in Pennsylvania compared to our pre-election poll; seven points better among Republicans in Ohio in the closing days of the race; three points better in North Carolina comparing Election Day to our last pre-election poll there.

In 2016 there was a widely held idea that Trump's deficit in the polls was somehow the result of pollsters missing hidden Trump voters outright—that is, not including them in polls. It turned out that some of them were very much in the polls already; they were Republicans hiding in plain sight.

If we think of campaigns like persuasion and marketing efforts, not races—and read the polls accordingly—we ask who might consider each candidate but isn't currently doing so. We ask how many of them there are. It's not just who's on board, it's who *might* join, and how easy or hard it is to imagine them joining. This is less a numerical calculation than assembling a profile of the whole electorate. These can include anyone who shares similar characteristics with the candidate's current backers. Republicans, in this case, were one of the largest and easiest segments for the Trump campaign to pick up. They were already partisan, and partisanship is a powerful draw. They agreed with him on a lot of issues. They told us in the polls they were not considering the Democratic alternative—and that may have been most telling of all. They were previously reliable voters. Seeing voters like this tells you that the campaign has room to change not because of a polling inaccuracy but because there is untapped potential market share.

The Late Break

The national-level 2016 polls turned out to be accurate by historical measures and showed Hillary Clinton up by nearly the same percentage by which she ultimately carried the national popular vote, though the important difference was that those national numbers did not decide the race, of course. Only the state races and the Electoral College did. The national polls were even more accurate than they'd been in 2012, when they actually underestimated the size of Obama's reelection win. Both the national vote and, from the evidence we have, state votes did show late shifts, however. Those shifts served as another reminder to think of election contests as collective decisions, not running tallies. When some pre-election polls did not show Trump with a lead, at least some of that was because he did not have one yet.

In Wisconsin, the second-to-last race we called, which put Trump close to the presidency, Trump won an astonishing 59 percent to 30 percent among people who decided in the last week. In Pennsylvania Trump won 53 percent to 37 percent of those who made their choice in the last few days.

Put that into vote terms: 10 percent of Pennsylvanians fell into that late-deciding camp, or 611,000 people. That gap of 53–37 percent among them netted Trump 97,000 votes. That's twice the amount by which he won the entire state: 44,000 votes. So the late breakers won him the race and the presidency, in that sense. The swings in the vote had come in the closing week and even in the final days.

The late-deciding voters in Wisconsin tended to be more conservative or moderate than liberal, in proportions much like the rest of the electorate. Trump voters there were almost twice as likely as Clinton's to say they decided in the final days. In Pennsylvania and Florida, they were slightly more likely to say that.

There was an explanation for why they decided late, too: they profiled as people who didn't like either candidate, but voted anyway. They said they voted on "the economy." In Wisconsin 60 percent of the late breakers rated it as their top issue and in Pennsylvania 51 percent did. But it was the decision on what to do about the economy that seemed to push them to Trump. In both cases majorities said their number-one priority was a candidate who could "bring about needed change." They fit the usual profile of a late-deciding voter who, the thinking usually goes, knows what the status quo is and if they haven't come around to supporting it by Election Day, never will.

Polling's Counter-Narratives

Every election cycle since I've been in the business, we seem to hear what one might call a counter-poll narrative, a theory expressed during the campaign—often by people other than pollsters—about why all the pre-election polls will ultimately turn out to be off. Usually it involves something that "the polls" (often unspecified) are missing. These fears don't always pan out, but they can be useful if we think of them as focusing attention on a problem before it happens. Pollsters can be a fastidious bunch when it comes to their estimates and quite mindful—some might say paranoid—about missing things, particularly something everyone said to watch out for.

In 2016, the narrative for Trump voters was that some of his backers didn't like the media and would decline to take our surveys altogether, or else they took the surveys but were embarrassed to tell the people conducting the survey they were voting for him. In 2008, a similar idea that voters were telling pollsters the wrong thing was imagined to be working in the opposite direction, with the idea that Barack Obama's poll number were false or inflated because people were just telling pollsters they'd vote for Obama in order to sound politically correct, particularly early in the primary season. Some speculated about the "Bradley effect," an idea that something similar had happened in the 1982 California governor's race with an African American candidate, Tom Bradley, who lost despite leading in the polls. My colleagues Sarah Dutton and Jen De Pinto had taken a hard look at this in our own surveys, and while they did find some signs that African American interviewers drew more respondents saying they'd vote for Obama, it wasn't a dramatic difference. Obama of course won both the nomination and the presidency after leading in the pre-election polls all fall.

In 2004, I remember people wondering if John Kerry would really beat George W. Bush even though he trailed in the polls, because supposedly young voters were missing from those surveys. The theory was that young people were using cell phones—the use of which was on the rise in those years—and not being polled. (We do call them today.) It didn't matter. That year the CBS News national poll had Bush and Vice President Dick Cheney up two points, and they won by two and a half. The poll actually *overstated* young support for Kerry, showing him with a twenty-point lead among them when, as it turned out, he won them by nine.

After the 2012 election, talk centered on why Mitt Romney and his polling team had reportedly believed that they would win. That appeared to be partly a turnout argument centering on that year's polls: people wondered if Democrats were being overstated and would not really turn out as they had in 2008, with the initial excitement of Obama's candidacy having faded and the economy still sluggish. I recall sitting on panel discussions in which pollsters traded back-and-forths over whether the polls had "too many Democrats" in them and hearing arguments that the electorate would end up being relatively older, or of less minority composition, in 2012. In fact, it seemed the opposite, at least in the national pre-election polls, which had shown a much tighter race than it really turned out to be when Obama won reelection.

Trump voters were not all hiding from pollsters in 2016, but the notion lingered all through the campaign, so we kept looking for signs that they were. I started by asking Trump supporters for descriptions of how the candidates made them feel, and the majority of Donald Trump's backers said "excited" and one-third of them said he made them feel "proud." When the idea first surfaced that perhaps people were too shy to talk about their support of Trump—that it might be politically incorrect to do so—we asked his early backers whether they were talking to friends and family about Trump, and a majority said they were talking out loud about their support, even telling others to vote for Trump, too. It sure didn't seem like there was a lot of shyness on their part, at least not in the ones who were taking our polls.

We'd polled throughout the primaries and we'd had Trump leading in thirteen out of fourteen in polls of Republican contests that he ended up winning. There wasn't a pattern from those polls in whether Trump tended to over- or underperform his pre-election surveys, as he actually split the fourteen evenly between doing better or worse than his specific pre-election estimates in our surveys. If Trump voters were consistently dodging polls en masse, he would have always outperformed his polling that spring.

Why Bother to Lie?

Still, the polling differences led some to wonder whether respondents outright lie about their vote preferences to pollsters. I think this speculation comes because most folks, being good and decent people themselves, don't realize how much effort it would take to lie, let alone for respondents to do so convincingly in a poll.

We all sometimes change how we talk in polite company. If someone is in polite company, though, chances are they want to be there, or have to be there, and so they have a stake in not offending anyone around them. But no one needs to be in a poll in the first place. It's not clear why someone would invest the time and energy of taking a poll at all, just to spend their time lying their way through it. It's more likely they would outright refuse to take the poll.

If they do take the poll, then, lying is really hard work. It takes more cognitive energy than just reflexively speaking from the gut.

The first thing such a respondent has to do is decide that they need to lie. That involves reminding themselves that they hold a view that others—in particular, those administering the survey—might find dislikable. Not everyone is that self-aware, and even if they are, they still simply may not care. Lying could be driven by a sense of obligation to be polite to a stranger, but then again there isn't much penalty for telling the truth there, because it is a stranger. And many polls—including our own state polls in 2016—are done online where respondents don't need to talk to an interviewer at all.

If the voters do decide they need to give a false answer, then they have the task of coming up with a substitute for their true feelings. To do that they need additional knowledge beyond their own views: they have to know what other people would find acceptable. That entails searching a little harder for an answer to give than simply expressing one's own feelings. This is the case for anyone telling a lie. There is an easier option on most surveys for the respondent to say they don't know or to decline to answer the question at all, which few respondents choose.

If they do take the dramatic step to say that they're voting for the *other* candidate, now their task gets harder still, because then they need to be consistent about their choices on other matters, or else it's going to be obvious they lied in the initial vote choice answer. So their other answers need to be in line with the initial lie; consistency is often what trips up most liars about anything.

If our supposed poll liar pretends to be a Clinton voter, to avoid suspicion they would need to pick the liberal or Democratic answers across the board for the rest of the survey, pretending to be something they aren't for all the other questions—including at the end where we ask demographic information or political ideology. That's a lot of role-playing without a lot of gain. If we'd seen a lot of "Clinton" voters in the polls who also wanted to build the wall with Mexico and repeal Obamacare and appoint conservative court justices, it would surely have raised our eyebrows.

I looked across all the surveys we did, and almost no one who said they were for Clinton went on to take even a bare handful of conservative or Trump-leaning positions across other questions when given the chance. None of them said Trump was better than Clinton on immigration, the economy, and terrorism.

Even if they had fibbed through those hurdles, 94 percent of them also said "no" when asked (because this was asked of all Clinton voters) if they'd ever consider voting for Donald Trump. If they were secretly backing Trump at that moment, that question would hardly have been a place to hold back.

Next I took a look through one of our larger studies, a multistate set of eleven battlegrounds in September, looking for other questions that might have baited out the disingenuous Trump voter. In one fun series, we'd asked people to go ahead and put themselves in the other side's shoes: for Clinton voters to tell us what they thought of Trump voters, and vice versa. Here, our Trump-voter-in-disguise would be given a chance to say something nice about Trump voters. If there was a group of liars among them, they didn't take the bait. Respondents who said they were backing Clinton described Trump supporters as people fooled by the New York businessman. When we asked what the result of a Clinton presidency would be, one of the choices was that the country would be damaged beyond repair. Fewer than 2 percent of Clinton voters in that survey picked that description, and of those few who did, they did not look like Republicans-in-hiding. Actually, many of them said they had actually voted in a Democratic primary, and most of them had voted for Obama in 2012.

If anything, the people in the polls who looked as if they were just paying lip service to the idea of voting for Clinton, but didn't really want to, the ones who expressed little enthusiasm for her, who didn't think her honest or had other negative things to say, didn't look like lying Trump voters. They were ex–Bernie Sanders backers.

•   •   •

National CBS News polls in the summer and fall of 2016 bounced up and down. They tightened toward Election Day. There was movement, particularly in Donald Trump's vote share, and it was when you'd expect based on events—dropping after times of controversy like the *Access Hollywood* bus tape and rising again as Republicans came back to him at the end. The national poll had the candidates even in September, Clinton leading by four and then nine in the middle of October, then back down to three at the start of November. If Republicans were refusing to take polls, or if polls consistently missed Republicans, you would be less likely to see that kind of movement. It looks instead like people just reacting to events. Some pollsters argued that this is caused by some voters shying away from taking polls temporarily, during times when their candidate is in trouble or going through a bad stretch. But these voters aren't always opposed to polls. On the other hand, the total percentage of Republicans in these national polls did not vary dramatically.

The Voters Who Didn't Show

We wondered how much our turnout estimates before the election had affected our state polls, as we'd spent the fall trying to figure out who was a likely voter and who was not. Had we done that right? We'd ended up seeing glaring turnout differences between some Republican and Democratic areas on Election Night. So in the days right after, we went back and recontacted the voters that we'd surveyed in all our pre-election polls in the battleground states to ask them what they'd really done on Election Day. We wanted to know if we'd really gauged their likelihood of voting correctly, or not.

It turned out we did well at gauging most of them in our polls, as best we could measure. Ninety-two percent of the people who told us they were *sure* to vote confirmed for us afterward that they *did*. Generally that's good in a polling estimate. In 2016 the election was so close that it had needed to be even better.

It's who decided *not* to vote that tells the tale: of the people who said, before the election, that they were *definitely* going to vote, but then after the election admitted they did *not* vote—in other words, they decided not to show up—Clinton had been their choice by 47 percent to 34 percent over Trump. By contrast, of the people who said they made good on their pre-election intent, telling us before the election that they definitely would vote, and then reporting they actually did, Trump took them by 45 percent to 42 percent. So among the people from our pre-election polls who ultimately didn't show up, Clinton had held more support. Comparably more of Clinton's pre-election backers overstated their likelihood of voting.

These people looked like a lot of otherwise reliable Democrats, not just would-be Clinton voters. Many had voted for Obama, but only eight in ten said they had voted for her in the end. It's another estimate that certainly might have flipped the race, and another reason why Clinton could not replicate the Obama coalition.

Our polls had included all those "definite" voters, and counted them as Clinton supporters, because they told us they'd vote and because they fit the profile of regular voters, too, having voted in the past. A pre-election poll is a portrait of people's preferences at the time. If they were wavering at the time we didn't pick that up. Then when they didn't show up, it affected the difference between the pre-election polling and the final results.

Overall, the people in battleground states who'd told us they were for Clinton—regardless of intention to turn out—reported showing up at a rate 2 percentage points less than Trump voters. It doesn't sound dramatic, nor is it enough to explain all the difference in the state polling, but it was enough to partly account for a swing in places.

While a lot of people assumed the polls had been missing Trump voters, here some polling differences could have come from an unwillingness by some Democrats to follow through with what they told pollsters.

I liked a line our correspondent Anthony Mason and producer Andy Wolff wrote on Election Night: "Republicans came home, and Democrats stayed home."

Some of the key differences were telling among core Democratic constituencies (though it was hardly confined to them). In the exit poll of Pennsylvania, for example, the African American percentage of the electorate dropped 3 percentage points from 2012, from 13 percent to 10 percent in 2016. I had, in one of my own October polls that showed a Clinton lead, also put it too high at 13 percent. Some months later, the Census completed its study of turnout nationwide, and reported that the turnout rate among African American voters declined for the first time in twenty years. It was the largest decline on record for blacks from one election to the next. A 2018 study by a group of political scientists estimated 4.4 million voters who had backed Obama in 2012 had stayed home, many of them white and over one-third of them black. It recalled the relative drop in turnout we saw on Election Night, especially in key cities like Milwaukee, Detroit, and Philadelphia, which almost certainly dropped Clinton's estimates from the pre-election polls down to the actual results. But this was not the single reason the contest turned out as it did or that the polls were "off"—particularly because there wasn't a lot of polling in those areas in the first place. It looked like one of many possible factors.

Also in those cities were a lot of young people, generally, and Clinton did worse with younger voters overall—another key part of the Democratic base—than Barack Obama had done. It was hardly confined to cities. With time after the election to formally piece all of it together, Doug Rivers looked at every county in America. He showed that in counties where the Republican typically does very well—where, say, Romney had decisively beaten Obama four years earlier—2016 turnout was up from 2012 as much as eight to ten points, which is a very substantial spike. In places where Democrats typically do well, where Obama had run up large margins over Romney, turnout was either down in 2016, or only up slightly, by just two points—either way, not nearly enough to offset that spike that came in Trump territory.

This difference was especially pronounced in the Upper Midwest states that swung the race. The exceptions were only places on the coasts where Clinton won especially big, like California and New York, which had strong turnout in Democratic counties but was of little help to Clinton's chances, running up the score in places it didn't matter electorally.

In 2018, the special counsel looking into possible Russian election interference indicted thirteen Russian nationals for meddling in the election, placing ads in social media, and creating false accounts. The Russia investigation took a sharp partisan turn in public opinion.

In our July 2017 survey among Republicans, who largely said they were not concerned about the allegations, half said they were unconcerned mainly because they felt it had not changed any minds or votes, and another one in five said they were not concerned because "in the end, Hillary Clinton was defeated." Democrats mostly said they were concerned because they felt it was a security risk and could happen again. At the end of 2017, eight in ten Republicans called the investigation politically motivated, while most Democrats called it justified.

But from a pollster's standpoint, the framework of this as it related to the election was whether or not those ads changed any minds or affected turnout, regardless of who was behind them. It was still not clear whether it did anything.

A study by a team of political scientists undertaken during the 2016 election looked at visits to "fake news" websites and found that the heavy users of those sites were already strongly pro-Trump. A relatively smaller number of Trump supporters read a great deal of fake news stories. The team doing the study described this as another sign that the "echo chamber," in which people reinforce existing beliefs, was deep but narrow. The study tracked users' trips to sites, although it wasn't clear what social media they had consumed.

We had checked in with voters self-reporting use of "social media like Facebook or Twitter" in one survey of battleground states Colorado, Wisconsin, Florida, and North Carolina in the summer of 2016. Half said they'd seen something about Clinton on those platforms, and just as many said they'd seen something about Trump. We didn't test whether it was good or bad. Of those who had seen things, the consideration of Clinton looked about the same as among those who'd reported seeing television ads and news reports. Forty-two percent of the ones not voting for Clinton said they would not have considered voting for any Democrat at all that year—and that was the same as among those who'd seen the other sources. The people using social media didn't report paying any more attention to the campaign than those looking at other sources. And in those states, at that time, anyway, they reported the same intended likelihood of voting.

When in Doubt, Do More Polls

We'd done over one hundred polls in the 2016 cycle all told, but we'd last polled Wisconsin six whole weeks before the election, and not again afterward. I hadn't done Michigan since the summer and I didn't poll Minnesota. If you looked at the preponderance of polls in the whole industry, the networks, the public pollsters, the universities, all were concentrated in places like Florida and Ohio but not the Upper Midwest. In its review of the 2016 polling, a panel of experts assembled by the American Association of Public Opinion Research suggested these Upper Midwest states had been under-polled by the entire industry, and called for more resources to do more high-quality surveys in places that weren't getting as much attention. So, just as our polling had been trending toward Trump in Ohio and Florida the final weekend, another look at the Midwest would have been warranted. And in the future you'll probably see more attention to trends across state lines.

Without new poll information, history tends to take over and people assume states will vote like they always do only to be surprised when things change. There were also two competing electoral narratives in 2016, one that went north and one that went south, which were equally compelling. On one hand was Trump's potential gains with white, working-class voters who concentrate in the North and the Rust Belt, on the other was Democrats' attempts to make inroads with the expanding suburbs of the higher-income, more diverse, growing Sun Belt states. Both happened to a degree, but the northern part of that story edged out and got its deserved attention because Trump won.

The shift in late deciders in 2016 made it especially glaring to everyone that the pre-election polling in the Midwest hadn't been sufficient; there was so little of it that was hard to really even label as good or bad; it just wasn't there. It might sound funny for the pollster to say it, but we need to do more polls.

I like to equate these lessons, taken together, as another reminder to break down any campaign as the campaign would (or should). Are there potential voters out there? This is more than just those labeled "undecided." This could well be people who seem sure of sitting out or picking another choice but are getting pressure to change. In this case, there were many Republicans who'd been loyal before. People may like the product—the candidate—but do they like it enough to act, to do something? There were some Democrats who did like Clinton, but not enough to get to the (physical) polls. And were there possible new areas? Those were clearly in the Midwest. If you frame what you look at in the electorate like a marketplace of people who might consider or might not consider a candidate, and a range of options for every voter type, you see things as a dynamic of possibilities rather than a single vote score. If you think in group terms to anticipate movement, you ask which groups— either through their stance on an issue, or their consideration of a candidate, or their past votes—might be likely to change their minds. Even better, ask yourself: If you were running the campaign, where are your weak spots, or who would you go after first? If things change, it'll probably end up explainable by something you already knew.

Chapter Five

What Are You Trying to Say?

If I walked into a cocktail party and saw my longtime friend Mike, I probably would not say:

"Hi, Mike! Are you doing well, or are you doing badly?"

That would make for an awkward start of a conversation. It would, however, make a good poll question.

It's balanced: it offers a range of possible answers and it doesn't take a side. In a normal conversational opening, if I'd just asked Mike if he was well, I probably *am* subtly signaling a bit of hope that he is. In a good poll question, we don't want to signal that we're hoping for anything.

The word "poll" comes from the Middle English word for head, or top. It came into usage as a shorthand for count—a head count—in medieval

Europe, enumerating how many by, naturally, counting heads. To a lot of us in the polling business, though, it's not always our favorite word for what we do. We often prefer the word "surveys," and call ourselves "survey researchers" to stress that we interview people, survey them, to understand how they think and feel, not just count them.

Finding just the right phrases to describe things isn't easy, as we "pollsters" have certainly learned. The math and the numbers get lots of attention for determining whether or not a poll is precise, but precision often starts with how we write the questions themselves, and what we make of them when we see the answers.

And the most important questions of a survey are the ones that pollsters ask themselves, before it starts. What do we really need to know? And just how do we measure that?

"Do you approve or disapprove of the way Ronald Reagan is handling his job as President?"

Consider the classic "presidential approval" question which has been in use for decades. (I used a historical name here just to underscore that this question has always been asked; only the names have changed over the years.) It's not phrased "Is Ronald Reagan doing a good job or not?" That could sound like there's a right answer out there somewhere. Asking "Do *you* approve . . . ?" right up front tells the respondent straightaway that we want *them* to be the ones to rendering judgment.

Nor do we ask "How good a job is Ronald Reagan doing?" That would presume it is good, and our query is just a matter of degree; as in, "*how* good?"

Be wary if you see that construction in poll questions, and it does show up from time to time. *"How concerned are you about a terrorist attack?"*

If I'm not, should I be? That phrasing could lead to some measurement error: we could report a slightly higher percentage of the public as being concerned than they really are, because the burden was on the respondent to negate the idea, as opposed to a nicely balanced, "Are you concerned or not concerned about a potential terror attack?" Then there's always the potential for a follow-up—"how concerned?"—with those who already are.

Sometimes the things we do to avoid biasing the answers are more subtle. In the presidential approval question the subject is not introduced as "President" so-and-so, but rather by name, then the job of president is specified later, "the way Ronald Reagan is handling his job as President." Some might think that's disrespectful but it's trying to be specific, and scientific. We're trying to measure what Americans think of the person's performance in the job, and if we had put the honorific in front of someone's name perhaps the respondent will feel they need to answer out of respect for the office regardless of the person in it, instead of their true feelings.

If we have to explain an idea that, unlike a president, might not be entirely familiar, we try to introduce it in as neutral a way as we can, and usually the fewer adjectives, the better.

"Do you favor or oppose building the Keystone XL pipeline that would transport oil from Canada through the United States to refineries in Texas?"

That can sound stilted and dry, but it avoids describing it in positive or negative terms or the implications either way. Just the facts, and preferably only the ones that would jog the memory of someone already familiar with the topic.

I did go back and find a real example that the poll asked in 1981, on another energy-related topic, that I don't think quite managed to avoid the problem: *"Would you favor increasing drilling for oil and natural gas off the California and Atlantic coasts, or do you think the risks of oil spills are too great?"*

There are risks of oil spills on one side of this question. But what are the benefits if you favor it?

• • •

What we get for a response can depend on _when_ we ask the question.

"Hey," my friend says around noon, "have you heard about the new study that shows sushi is dangerous to eat?"

"No, I didn't," I answer.

"So let's get lunch," he says. "Do you want Chinese food or Japanese food?"

Guess which I'll probably pick.

I actually haven't seen any such study. But his first question probably affected how I thought about the second one, if not how I answered it outright. On a pre-election poll, the main vote choice questions, who are you voting for, come before we ask whether you think the candidates are honest or competent. The presidential approval question is always asked before we ask how the president is doing on specific items like the economy or foreign policy. Whichever of those is fresh in the respondent's head when the main approval question comes up could affect how they think.

Measure questions like _"Do you think the war is going well or going badly"_ start a string of questions on the war and don't come after a question like _"How much have you heard about the recent U.S. gains on the battlefield?"_—there you would be giving people information they might or might not have—or even _"How long do you think the war will last?"_ which could become the specific framework that's in respondents' minds for how they evaluate the war overall.

When we ask a vote question, or most anything with a list such as— _"If the presidential Election were being held today, would you vote for John Kerry, the Democrat, or George Bush, the Republican"_—there might be some respondents who are more inclined to pick the first name on a list, and some who would pick the last thing they heard. So we randomly rotate the order in which the candidates are listed as we go through the interviews. A random half of poll respondents get the question with Kerry's name first and Bush's name second, and a random half get Bush and then Kerry. Over time and over the course of all the interviews, any order effects for having been listed first or second, for either candidate, should cancel out.

All Sorts of Questions

As congressional Republicans geared up to pass their tax bill in late 2017, the obvious question to ask on our survey was whether or not people thought they'd get a tax cut. It turned out few people thought they would get a cut at the time, and only half of Republicans thought they would.

Had we stopped there and only inferred that people didn't like the bill—that is, that they *evaluated* it badly—because they weren't getting a cut, we'd have been wrong.

It turned out that Republicans' opinions of the bill were nonetheless quite positive, and a lot more of them supported the bill than thought they'd get a tax cut from it. Some of those responses were driven by partisanship, of course. Others believed that it would help the larger economy, and them only indirectly. But the key for the pollster is making sure we have different question types that distinguish between what people think is factually true about something, and what their own opinion of it is. There's a difference.

In their straightforwardly named book *Asking Questions*, Norman Bradburn, Seymour Sudman, and Brian Wansink summarize a helpful way to think of question types, describing the three components of respondents' attitudes: "cognitive, evaluative, and behavioral."

The cognitive is what you believe is true about an object or person. (Whether it is or isn't.)

The evaluative is how you personally feel about it.

And the behavioral is what you would do about it.

For example:

From what you've heard, how far do you think electric cars can go on a charge?

How much of the new tax cut goes to the middle class?—

That's what you think is true about those topics.

Do you like electric cars?

Do you approve of the new tax cut?—

That's asking your personal feelings about them.

Will you buy an electric car?

Will you vote for a congressman who backs the tax cut?—

That's asking what action you might take.

Bradburn and his coauthors caution that we cannot conflate these when we're putting together a survey. We might learn that people now believe (as a fact) that electric cars can drive for hundreds of miles on a charge. That doesn't mean they like the car. People might dislike the cars in spite of knowing that they have better range, maybe because they're too small, or because of some other feature we haven't measured. And if they do like the car, that doesn't mean they'll buy one. We don't know that unless we ask if they can afford it, or if they're even in the market for a car in the first place.

And then of course there's what people will or won't do about it. For example, we could ask: *"Would you be more likely to vote for a Congressional candidate who thought it was more important to cut taxes, or for a Congressional candidate who thought it was more important to balance the budget?"*

Meanings and Symbols: The National Anthem Controversy

In the fall of 2017 President Trump chastised NFL players for kneeling during the national anthem, sparking a further wave of protests in football stadiums that September. *The New York Times* wrote, "What had been a modest round of anthem demonstrations this season led by a handful of African-American players mushroomed and morphed into a nationwide, diverse rebuke to Mr. Trump, with even some of his staunchest supporters in the N.F.L., including several owners, joining in or condemning Mr. Trump for divisiveness."

So we put together a survey on Americans' reactions. Even though it was a controversy, I did not want to ask a question that directly had people choose a side between the players and the president. That would have been forcing a construct onto people. I wanted separate measures for what they thought of each, because it was possible they thought both were right—or neither.

So the first question was:

"Do you approve or disapprove of Donald Trump's recent comments about football players who protest during the national anthem?"

And I offered a scale for approval and disapproval: "strongly" approve or just "somewhat" approve, for those who did approve. This was one of those topics some people would surely feel passionate about, and indeed that was the case. Most who had a view had a strongly held one.

Then: *"Do you approve or disapprove of football players protesting by kneeling during the national anthem?"*

The phrase "taking a knee" would probably have been familiar to sports fans, but maybe not to others. If people don't know a phrase, they might skip the question or—worse—answer it anyway, and answer differently than they would have had they understood it.

And it turned out that most people didn't like either side's actions, neither the kneeling nor the president's involvement.

Subject matter like the anthem and the flag led us to wonder: what did those things symbolize to people in the first place? There were clearly bigger themes at work here: race, patriotism, the military, the presidency, and a communal institution, football games. How people already felt about those might be driving their views on the whole controversy.

So I needed benchmarks and asked, "To you, personally, does the flag and national anthem represent . . ." Then a yes/no list of items that the flag might symbolize. One was whether the flag did (or did not) represent "the right to free speech anytime"; "loyalty to the government"; "the military and veterans who've fought for the country"; "traditions that should be honored." I kept the last two separate because it was possible that both sides of this controversy would believe that they were honoring traditions—just different ones: one side, by saluting the military, the other by speaking up. (And in fact they did.) It turned out that large majorities of Americans felt the flag and anthem represented most of those things, but least of all "loyalty to the government."

I talked with reporters covering the story and one reminded me that we ought not to assume everyone knew the whole backstory to the controversy and where it had originated in the first place, which was with now ex–San Francisco quarterback Colin Kaepernick protesting police treatment of African Americans. In the act of kneeling, there was no outward expression from the players saying what they were protesting, no banners or signs decrying police behavior or racism. So in thinking about the poll questions, one could imagine a viewer who hadn't tuned in until now, just seeing players kneeling and not knowing why they were doing so. Being unaware of the protest could affect their responses, a case where we wanted to know what people thought was objectively true, separate from their own evaluations of it.

I asked: *"Whether or not you agree with them, what do you feel the football players' protests are trying, or not trying, to do?"*

Then I gave a yes/no list including: "disrespect the flag and anthem itself"; "call attention to racism"; "call attention to unfair police tactics"; "disrespect the military and veterans."

When the results came in, only one-third of Americans thought the players were trying to disrespect the military and fewer than half, four in ten, thought they were trying to disrespect the flag itself. So the majority likely did know what the aim of the protests was. And it turned out that perceptions of motivation were indeed associated with views on the kneeling. The people who said they knew the aim of the protests—those who said the players were trying to call attention to racism—were more approving than those who did not. There were some, four in ten, who did not think the players were trying to disrespect the flag, but who disapproved of the protests anyway.

The people who thought the players *were* trying to disrespect the flag, or trying to disrespect the military, were unsurprisingly not okay with protests at all: almost nine in ten disapproved of their actions.

Both those views were also in turn highly correlated with partisanship, and the bulk of those who disapproved were Republicans, suggesting that both the president and his supporters were taking cues from each other on this.

For balance and for explanation, we asked what Americans thought of the president's motivations; why he'd spoken out.

"Whether or not you agree with him, what do you feel Donald Trump is trying to do with his comments about the football players?"

Was he trying to unite the country by telling everyone to respect the flag, divide the country by singling people out, or did he not have a larger purpose with it at all?

The answers came back split among the three. Those who backed the players thought the president was trying to divide the country, and those who disapproved of the protests thought the president was trying to unify the country. The splits by race were notable, as African Americans read the situation very differently from many whites and from Republicans in particular. African Americans were nearly as likely to feel that the president's comments were intentionally divisive and singling out people as conservative whites were to think that his comments were a genuine attempt to unify the country by getting everyone to respect the flag.

Asking questions about motivation helped explain why we saw the demographic differences that we did.

Survey questions aim to figure out not just what people think, but what they mean, and how they feel.

Chapter Six

What's the Story?

"Do you believe in ghosts?"

Yes, the CBS News poll asked about that in October 2011. As it turned out, 40 percent of Americans say they do. But that is not a ghost story.

It's not really a story at all. It's just a fact. I hear it, and I want to know more. Have people seen one? If so that would be interesting: millions of ghost sightings in America. Are parts of our country haunted? Some more than others? That would surely be good to know. Or maybe a lot of people who believe in ghosts haven't seen one, in which case we learn something about how people think, and what they're willing to believe without any visual or personal evidence. Either way, if we knew any of those things, we'd start to learn something larger about people—which is what really interests us here. Now we'd have a story.

Good polls—surveys—do exactly that, take a series of questions, all aimed at different ideas and aspects of a topic, and weave them together to tell us a larger tale about ourselves, or how our politics works, and why we see the results we see.

(And of course, my colleagues who did that ghost study anticipated all of this because they're first-rate researchers. It turns out that half of everyone who believes in ghosts does claim to have seen one. And yes, Americans said that to a pollster. It adds up to millions who've been haunted. I'm sure they have a lot of stories to tell.)

The most revealing sets of questions show something you genuinely didn't know—but maybe should have.

Hillary Clinton kept stressing the commander-in-chief test between herself and Donald Trump: she argued that she knew more, that she was qualified, and that he was not. For a while it seemed like that particular message was working. We asked whether each of them was prepared to be commander in chief and in a lot of states she led on that measure by more than twenty points. But this was odd and nagging: then why didn't she have a bigger overall lead in the campaign? There are a host of possible reasons, of course, but one seemed especially glaring. She was focused on her qualifications—knowledgeable, experienced—all of which were attributes that accrued to her. Even her detractors in the polling said they thought she knew more than her opponent. All this was looking like a classic problem in Marketing 101 of attributes versus benefits.

Attributes describe the thing you're buying, but what people really want to know is, What does it do for me? As a friend in market research once put it, an attribute of a car is that it has a great engine. The benefit of that car to you, the consumer, is that it helps you get where you're going faster. The latter matters more.

So I included another question in our Battleground Tracker polls in the fall of 2016: Which candidate would make you feel safe?

After all, it was implied, isn't that the reason you want the commander in chief to have all those qualifications? Not for their sake, but for yours.

On this issue the two candidates were often even. In some states more people thought Trump would keep them safe. And in the final calculus, respondents who thought Trump was unprepared for the job, but nonetheless felt he would keep them safe, were voting for him by a five-to-one margin. Whatever it was that brought on the feeling, safety was what mattered.

It was a reminder not to assume meaning from one polling question when you can find a way to let people tell you how they're feeling instead.

Feelings behind the Gun Debate

By the end of 2017, a year in which a Las Vegas gunman killed fifty-eight and left more than five hundred injured; a gunman in a West Texas church had killed more than two dozen; gun violence in other cities routinely made news; and the nation marked the five-year anniversary of the Sandy Hook school massacre in Newtown, Connecticut, seven in ten Americans called gun violence at least a very serious problem and a third of them called it a crisis. In early 2018, a Florida school would see a mass shooting lead to a massive march fueled by student organizers in Washington, D.C., that spring, igniting the debate over guns once more.

Few things simultaneously spark passions and frustrations on all sides like the argument over guns, and it's a prime example of an issue where policy and public opinion often diverge and leave every side saying they're frustrated. (That is, in fact, the most picked feeling that both gun owners and gun control advocates each use to describe the situation.)

Guns obviously represent something more personal than just a policy position, and we wondered if we could measure those feelings more precisely, to understand how people saw the broader role guns played in the country and what might help us explain how those divisions became so hardened.

In late 2017, I put together a survey of both gun owners and non-owners, with an intentionally and disproportionately large group of gun owners included—a standard technique called an oversample. I began by thinking of words that I'd heard people on either side of the gun debate use in describing guns' impact on the country. I put some of them to respondents, giving them the chance to pick any, all, or none.

> *"Guns make America . . . Free? Dangerous?*
> *Safe? Scary? Strong? Uncivilized?"*

We got opposing descriptions from gun owners and non-owners. Most gun owners felt guns made America "free" (61 percent), "strong" (55 percent), and "safe" (59 percent). Most non-gun-owners said they made America "dangerous" (55 percent) and then many even picked "scary" (38 percent), both of which jumped to higher numbers among women. In another question I offered more of a chance at hyperbole, and many took it, with the majority of gun owners saying guns were part of what "makes America great." Non-gun-owners by contrast were more apt to call guns one of the country's biggest problems.

A lot of polling on guns often takes place after mass tragedies, a lot of it revolves around preferences for stricter laws; preferences that don't necessarily go up that much after shootings. The longer-term trend over the decade has been only a slight rise in the percentage who call for stricter laws in general, and six in ten support the idea in general, as of 2017, though the specifics of what stricter means quickly send people into their respective camps. The gender gap on the matter is striking, though, as more than two-thirds of women back stricter laws and fewer than half of men do. Those who feel guns make America a "scary" or "dangerous" place are disproportionately women, and women with young children in particular. The divide is sharply partisan, too, with eight in ten Democrats calling for stricter measures but only three in ten Republicans agreeing—though more Republicans would leave restrictions as they are, not lessen them.

I wanted to know whether proponents and opponents of gun control even believed the problem could be addressed in the first place, so I asked if mass shootings were preventable, or if they were an unfortunate but inevitable part of a free society, and half of gun owners picked the latter. The other half said they were preventable, though, as did most non-gun-owners.

We asked gun owners the main reason they owned guns, and to them safety was paramount. The largest number said it was for defending themselves from crime, by more than three to one over other items like hunting, and by more than the reasons of hunting, tradition, and sport shooting combined.

Next, I wanted to have a place for people to express just what it was they needed protection from. Because other surveys have shown the same desire for protection, we could anticipate that answer coming up, and this was a chance to explore it further. We asked what potential physical threat concerned them, and an overwhelming 87 percent picked criminals, muggers, and thieves. A majority 60 percent added terrorists. One in five said it was the threat of domestic violence or someone they knew. A sizable four in ten picked rioters as a threat, and nearly one-third of city dwellers selected that, as did most of those in rural areas. I included things like government officials as potential threats on the list because sometimes armed, antigovernment groups make the news, and I wondered whether or to what degree that was a stereotype. Relatively few gun owners, 20 percent, picked it.

To try to get at just how secure the gun made them feel, I asked how well people felt they could handle and resolve a conflict if they actually had to engage and use the weapon. I didn't go so far as to ask if they'd shoot someone or could hit a target, but I used the phrase "resolve the situation," which I think conveyed the proper idea. Were they very or somewhat confident? Or were they not very confident, but at least feeling like the gun gave them a fighting chance. I offered that latter "fighting chance" option explicitly in the last answer code, because people don't normally like to undersell their abilities about anything, so the inclusion evened out the question by offering a way for someone to admit uncertainty without conceding too much.

The results, though, came back to show gun owners were expressly confident. Most felt at least somewhat confident that they could resolve a situation outright if they needed to use the gun. That told a story: it helped undergird that feeling of safety that gun ownership brings to them.

Gun debate arguments in support of gun rights often move from ideas of practical defense to larger ideas and language that center on rights and liberty. We gave everyone in the survey a list of constitutional rights—speech, religion—including the right to bear arms, and asked them to describe how important each was in their day-to-day lives. For gun owners, the right to bear arms ranked as important to them as freedom of religion, exceeded only by freedom of speech. These are ideas that by definition have personal meanings, so next I asked gun owners what the gun itself represented to them personally. Along with protection, they said freedom, most also said "responsibility."

Because I'd offered the word "responsibility," I then added another question to try to unpack a bit of what that specifically entailed. For instance, did they think weapons training ought to be required for gun ownership, like—and I put the direct comparison right in the question—"taking a driving test to get a driver's license?" Most said yes, it should.

I wanted to check on the possible pervasiveness of stereotypes, so

I added very direct questions about the presumed motives of gun control and gun rights groups'. It was striking how differently, and with such mistrust, gun rights proponents saw the motives of gun control advocates—and vice versa. Some of the questions leaned toward hyperbole, but that was partly the point, because political dialogue and rhetoric often does, too, so why not see if it's true or false in the public mind.

A full two-thirds of gun owners said they believed that gun control groups were out to take away "all guns, period." And three-fourths of everyone who opposed stricter gun laws worried that any new laws would lead to that. Six in ten also felt gun control groups were trying to change people's traditions and ways of life, and give government more control over people, generally. This was especially true among those who did not support stricter laws.

Non-gun-owners, though, didn't see it that way. There was no push for getting rid of all guns from non-gun-owners. Only 18 percent of people who did not themselves own guns thought the country would be safer if no one owned guns. Only one-quarter of people who did not own guns and thought laws ought to be stricter defined gun control efforts as a push to take away all guns. Most of them saw gun control as trying to promote public safety, and few saw it as about control or tradition at all.

Meanwhile, a majority who don't own guns, and want stricter laws, feel that gun owners are trying to arm themselves for "a larger and more violent conflict." Half of them felt that gun rights groups were thinking about "arming themselves against the government." Did people see the argument over guns as dovetailing with racial views or racial animosity? Half thought gun rights groups were making a racial or cultural statement with their push for gun rights. Far fewer, under a quarter of gun owners opposed to stricter laws, actually said that they were.

It was clear that to some degree, in the political dialogue at least, the sides are clearly talking past one another or at least filled with outright suspicion about the other.

This, despite the fact that there is an agreement on some of the causes of gun violence, beyond guns themselves. Most of the agreement connects to ideas of individual behavior, where both gun and non-gun-owners assign blame. Background checks, to rule out criminals and terrorists, are universally favored, in principle, because they take action against bad actors rather than the weapon. (Gun owners expressed concern, however, about implementation, that the government would keep a database of people and their purchases.) Mental health screenings and treatment initiatives find common agreement as ways to reduce violence, and the idea that gun violence is perpetrated by criminals, drug dealers, and gangs, all cut across party lines and stances on gun laws. As does the idea that current laws are not enforced. Those agreements, when seen in the aggregate polling numbers, often lead people to wonder why at least some additional steps aren't taken, and the mistrust between the sides is clearly one reason.

The political and voting explanations of what happens to gun policy often amount to a shorthand idea of a "single-issue voter," one who focuses only on one policy—in this case, guns—and one whom the politicians won't cross, and won't enact more gun restrictions for fear of crossing. That leads gun control groups to express the belief—and often dismay—that wider public support for their views is counteracted by a smaller but much more politically effective group of gun rights backers, who exert outsize influence not just because of their stance but because of the unified actions they'll take at the ballot box.

Can we use polling to measure that, or see if it's actually true?

We asked people what they did politically in support of their views on gun policy. Gun owners reported in 2017 that they took actions at a higher rate, such as contacting their member of Congress and donating money to sympathetic causes at twice the rate of non-owners.

Then we asked very simply: Which are issues where a candidate simply must agree with you to win your vote, and which are issues where you could disagree, but still vote for someone? For gun owners, gun policy was tops on their must-have list. Three-quarters would rule out voting for any candidate who didn't agree with them. If we then further segment out the gun owners who feel gun restrictions should be maintained or lessened, in particular, that litmus-test figure jumps to more than eight in ten. (It is, by the way, higher than the rate at which these mostly conservative voters would rule out a candidate on abortion, just to compare guns to another hot-button issue.)

The same single-issue focus on guns just isn't as high among non-gun-owners. It's lower, by double digits.

Gun owners who say any candidate must agree with them on guns: 74 percent.

Non-owners who say any candidate must agree: 61 percent.

Then three-quarters of gun owners who also want less restrictive gun laws say they've voted *strictly* based on the issue. The percentage of non-owners who want tougher laws that have voted singularly on the gun issue? It's just 17 percent. So that dramatic difference stood out.

Percentage of gun owners who want fewer restrictions—who have voted only based on gun policy: 74 percent.

Percentage of non-owners, who want more restrictions—who have voted only based on gun policy: 17 percent.

That is what measuring outsize influence looks like, the difference between the larger percentages you see in national polls and the policy output.

That is what single-issue voting looks like, quantified. That's what two groups with misconceptions about each other look like. And that's a better story—about how politics works in real life—than just a percentage.

Chapter Seven

How to Learn a Lot from a Little

Suppose you're taking the whole extended family to the movies, a big sprawling group of people, and it's your turn to pick what to see. But you've got a lot of picky people of assorted tastes to please, especially if your wacky brother shows up, and you'll never hear the end of it if they don't all have a good time.

So you've narrowed it down to a choice of two new releases, both dramatic thrillers, let's say one is titled *The Last Call*, and the other is *The Pollster Always Rings Twice*. You look at one of those review websites where moviegoers have rated them each from zero to five stars, and see that each gets an average rating of 4.

The Last Call: Average Rating = 4.
The Pollster Always Rings Twice: Average Rating = 4.

So at first glance it seems like you've got two good options, and you can pick either one and please the crowd.

But which? Can we make a more informed decision? Let's look and see if we can learn something more, and fast. The kids are getting rambunctious and you haven't the time or inclination to read through all the comments of reviews; plus you think those can be tedious, anyhow. People seem to like movies for such an assortment of reasons.

Maybe just the data can still teach us something.

Scrolling through the ratings for *The Last Call*, with its 4-star average, you see it gets a lot of 5-star ratings mixed in to that, the highest rating allowed. That's a good thing! Then you see it also gets a handful of 1 ratings, the lowest rating allowed. The pattern in fact looks like this:

5,5,5,5,5,5,5,5,5,5,5,5,5,5,5,1,1,1,1,1 (Average = 4)

One story you could tell from this data is that *most* people really love *The Last Call*. *Most* gave it a 5-star rating. In fact, if you were in advertising and you had to sell the movie, that might be exactly what you'd say. You have a different task, though. You need to know precisely what to expect from the movie, what your crowd will think of it. Now look at the whole set of data and you learn something more important to your situation: that whenever people don't like it, they really hate it. They gave it 1s! There isn't much in between.

So if you take someone to see *The Last Call*, chances are they'll love it, but if they don't, they'll be very displeased. The real story here is that *The Last Call* is a love-it-or-hate-it movie.

Then you look at the ratings for *The Pollster Always Rings Twice* and you see they look like this, a perfectly consistent string of 4 ratings, with nary a best-possible 5, nor a lowly 1, in sight. It's got the same average overall as *The Last Call*, but it got there with a consistent pattern.

4,4,4,4,4,4,4,4,4,4,4,4,4,4,4,4,4,4,4,4 (Average = 4)

The Pollster Always Rings Twice, by virtue of that consistency, looks like more of a sure bet about what kind of reaction you're going to get from anyone you take to see it. While no one absolutely loves it and ranks it best, neither does anyone hate it outright. You know you've got that big group of people to take to the movie, and you don't want to disappoint anyone. It seems like surely someone in your big group would probably end up hating the more polarizing *Last Call*—since a quarter of everyone who rates that movie does indeed hate it. Whereas with *The Pollster*, with its consistent, reliable 4s, you have a much better idea of what to expect. Chances are everyone will at least like it, and that no one will say they had a horrible time.

So you pick that one. Everyone has fun, you're the hero, and you made a good decision just by using the spread of the data.

I gave these two movies the same average to emphasize a point. If we set out to measure something, be it movie reviews, or opinions, or a candidate's vote share in a state, getting measurements that cluster tightly together every time we look makes us more confident in our description of it. We know what to expect. Seeing a wider spread—or distribution— makes us less confident. Either way, we've learned more than we could have just from looking at the one number alone, the average.

We put this idea to work in polling a lot.

Make the Call in Alabama

I had not expected to be paying attention to Alabama in December of 2017. Or any year, for that matter, because we usually know what will happen there and why. It's so reliably Republican that any statewide candidate with an "R" next to their name is going to win easily, get a big majority of the white vote, almost none of the African American vote, and turnout won't be especially high. Trump had won the state by thirty points. When Jeff Sessions left his Alabama Senate seat—to which he'd been reelected unopposed—and became attorney general, the state called a special election to choose his replacement. The Republican nominee for it, Judge Roy Moore, was accused of making advances on underage girls when he was in his thirties, and prominent national Republicans including Senate Majority Leader Mitch McConnell had called for him to quit the race. Moore denied the allegations and stayed in as a handful of early polls showed him trailing the Democrat, Doug Jones. Jones ultimately edged Moore by just over a point in a race that drew national coverage.

But just who would vote in this election? Special elections take place at odd and idiosyncratic times, like this one, coming before the holidays in an odd-numbered year. The pre-election polls had bounced around. Some had Jones up double digits, some had Moore up, and the race clearly depended on turnout: whether the Democrats and Republicans could get their voters to show up for the first really competitive state race in years.

On Election Night, things are tight between Jones and Moore from the outset. County reports start coming in and the lead in our statistical models seesaws between the two, then Jones takes a slight lead. We're at the Decision Desk again—this time, for single-state coverage, and we're sitting upstairs from the CBS studio. County after county reports its votes, but there's one big county missing, Jefferson, which is heavily Democratic, important to Jones's chances, and too big to ignore. We could make assumptions about it based on its past votes, but we'd rather make an informed choice from what we're seeing tonight. So we're on the phone trying to get the results from our reporters there, but nothing more seems to be coming. It's a nail-biter. The question is whether we can call this race as a narrow win for Jones without it.

So we look at the data from all the other Democratic-leaning counties that have votes reported in: similar places, so they're the best for comparisons. In all of them, turnout is up from what we'd expected, and consistently. We run down the list: Macon, up 18 percent; Bullock, up 18 percent, Wilcox, up 17 percent; and so on. None of those figures are varying a lot. The data keeps showing us the same thing over and over, so Jefferson—still missing—probably has that same double-digit turnout bump. If those other counties had been a mixed bag of reports, some high and some low, we would have kept on waiting.

We make the call for Jones. (Later, Jones does eventually see an 18 percent increase in Jefferson when it reports, almost exactly what we'd expected.)

There are plenty of times we all use consistency to make decisions in our real day-to-day lives, too. On your morning commute, if you need to stick to a schedule, you'll pick a street where you can regularly time the traffic over the road that's sometimes totally clear but sometimes totally jammed. If you're going on vacation to San Diego in April, where the temperature rarely seems to vary much from 72 degrees, you'll pack differently (and be more confident you're prepared) than if you're going to New York in April, where it can easily go from 40 degrees to 70. Though we all tend to remember unusual events that we see, and out-of-the-ordinary stories of things that happen to us, when we need to describe how the world *really* is, it's consistency we look for and value.

Rick's Café Américain

Okay, work is done for a moment, let's go back to the movies. This time, let's see a real one, a classic.

Early on in *Casablanca*, we see that Rick Blaine, played by Humphrey Bogart, has a soft spot in his heart despite all his tough talk. It's in the casino, at the roulette table. (And shortly before Captain Renault will be "shocked, shocked" to find gambling going on.)

Rick, who runs the casino, decides to help a young man who's down on his luck and desperately trying to find the money to get himself and his fiancée out of town. The young man is sitting at the roulette wheel, losing. Rick approaches him and says, "Have you tried 22 tonight?" After a long glance, the young man gets the hint, and puts his money on 22 black. It comes up and he wins.

The young man reaches to collect his money. "Leave it there," Rick commands. The wheel spins again, letting his bet ride on 22. Everyone is silent. And then the white ball lands . . . on 22 again!

The crowd murmurs. A woman stands up and asks, with a hint of outrage, "Are you sure this game is honest?" Renault looks over, suspiciously.

"He's just a lucky guy," Rick says, but watching the scene, we all know Rick is lying—albeit for a good cause.

How do we know this game is rigged, and more importantly, how do we know so quickly? It's obvious to the audience from the interplay of Rick and the croupier at the roulette wheel, of course, and in the knowing looks they exchange. But we would suspect this anyway, just from the statistics. We know what the probabilities of selection are for each number that could come up. One win on a single-number bet for this young man would normally be astounding luck, a 1 in 37 chance on a European-style roulette wheel. But like the woman who immediately jumps up, if we think of the young man's picks as a set, we also instinctively know that the odds that 22 will come up twice in a row are enormous, bordering on the ridiculous. We don't even need to compute them in our head at over a thousand to one.

Here's what we instinctively knew in a sampling sense: that the numbers on Rick's roulette wheel were not picked fairly, in this case, randomly. If it had been random, then we would not likely have seen something really unusual. We would not have seen someone bet 22 twice and win. Even more importantly, it didn't take long for us to see this. We didn't need to wait to see 22 come up dozens of times in a row. That's because we know that randomness *quickly* rules out the unlikely result.

Hang on to that instinct. You can use it to think about a concept that underpins random sampling, and why we use polling samples of 500 to 1,000 people to form our little microcosms of the country. We already know that we're assembling the country in miniature, that we can put together a representative cross section of America, but what makes the number 1,000 so magical when we're doing that? Why not 10? Or 100,000? Or 1,000,000?

If you listen to pollsters when they're working you'll hear them use the phrase "drawing" a sample, or "pulling a sample," as we go about assembling our world-in-miniature. Of course we don't literally yank people out of their homes. This is language derived from the process that gives a random sample its power, the act of picking it piece by piece.

Suppose that theater chain hired you to find out what percentage of Americans consider themselves movie fans. Let's suppose the answer out there is that half of Americans are, even though we can't see that fact before we start.

Now assume for a moment that we can pick someone for our poll from among everyone in America. Never mind how we'll interview them. Assume we'll be entirely fair—unlike Rick's roulette wheel—picking without favoritism; and without picking anything deliberately because of what we thought it might do to the composition of the sample. Nor do we ever want to systematically *exclude* people simply because of the way we made our choices.

Here's what will emerge: Because half of those people out there really are movie fans—again, pretend we don't know this yet, but that it is true—we would have a 50/50 chance to get a fan into our sample with that first blind, fair-to-everyone pick. Now, we do it again. We pick another person, and again we have a 50 percent chance to pick a movie fan on that second pick, too, and a 50 percent chance for a nonfan, because those are the proportions really out there in the population.

Building up our sample pick by pick this way, we can already start to see how this is going to play out as we pick over and over. You almost surely won't get a sample *dominated* by either fans or nonfans by drawing it randomly. That process of repetition means over time we are going to pull fans as often as we pull nonfans, and roughly 50 percent of the time each, because there are the same number of each. Doing that picking again and again and again as we assemble our sample means that reality—the fact that half of the people are fans—is going to be reflected in our sample very quickly.

We would not expect to have a wild imbalance of people who hold atypical views in anything, any more than we'd expect our young man in Casablanca would really have kept winning. In our poll the chances of pulling out just five people in a row without getting any movie fans would be less than one in twenty. Even Rick Blaine might be shocked if we did that.

So what's average in the real world is roughly what emerges in your sample, because each time you select someone you'll tend to pick the people who are driving that population average in the first place.

Then imagine how unlikely it would be if we were to take whole samples, one whole sample after another, only to find that each of those entire samples was itself dominated by an unusual result, like samples with just movie fans, or just nonfans. Instead, when we select people randomly, put those picks into samples, and then draw samples over and over, what we get from all of them will tend toward what's average for the population, and away from what's unusual for the population. The mathematical expression of this idea is called the central limit theorem.

It's what we suspected even before we started calculating odds: that randomness works fast. The average-looking samples start quickly outnumbering the unusual ones as we draw. Our samples converge around the true average of the population.

Here's a look at what really happened when we sampled in one of our polls for a population percentage that we already knew, also one that's about evenly divided, men and women. Women are 52 percent of the adult population, per the Census. If I pull out a CBS News poll from 2013 and look at it unweighted and unadjusted, meaning this is just the result from the sampling, the poll is 51 percent female. A poll from 2014: 51 percent female. A poll from 2017: 50 percent female. We got around the right number (though not always *exactly* the right number, as you can see) again and again. We did not get samples with something way off, such as with 20 percent women in them, or 100 percent women, either.

With opinions, though, we don't have a Census to compare to. There is no Official Movie Census to tell us 50 percent of people like movies. We can do a poll on what Americans think of a new tax plan, but there's no instant tally at that exact moment for all 300 million people's opinions to compare it with. That's why we did the poll in the first place. If this were archery, we'd just aim at the bull's-eye and measure how many inches away our arrow hit. In opinions we never know where the bull's-eye is when we start.

Yet we do know that drawing our samples in a random way rules out the unusual and gets them close to true values. So then the question just becomes how much sample it takes to get us close, and how confident we can be that we've found what we're looking for when we're done. This is where the margin of error will come in.

For that, we'll need to think in terms of certainty.

Why 1,000, Anyway?

And so we turn to San Francisco detective Harry Callahan, otherwise known as Dirty Harry.

"You've got to ask yourself one question . . ." Harry says. "Do I feel lucky? Well . . . do ya, punk?"

We all know the scene. Harry is standing there at the end of a shoot-out, his .44 Magnum pointed, and we don't know whether Harry's got a bullet left in his gun, or if the gun is empty. The audience knows Harry's question isn't really about luck at all, it's just a fun way to pose the question.

Harry's question is about confidence. Are we sure he has a bullet? Or not sure? This is the question that matters, and there is a true, existing answer to it regardless of what we think or what we guess in this moment.

Notice that no one in this scene seems concerned with accuracy, in the sense that Harry's not talking about *aim*. He might not know exactly, down to the millimeter, where his shot would go, but that seems irrelevant to him; he won't miss entirely. This story hinges on a yes-or-no question.

Think about a margin of error like Harry might. There's a correct percentage out there to be found. Do you think you've got something close enough to it, or not? Do you feel . . . confident?

We approached the sample using the idea that probability would help us find the right number to describe our population. We don't know what that right number is, exactly. But we can also use probability to judge our chances of having found it. Pollsters typically set their criteria for being confident such that the true population value, that truth we're after—like the fact that about half of Americans are women—would be within range of our poll result 95 out of 100 times we repeated the poll. Then the more people we talk to, the narrower that range becomes. This will lead us to what we call our margin of error. We know with our sampling we can quickly rule out the really unusual, but then getting closer around the truth takes more samples.

The good news is that the range starts to narrow quickly as probability goes to work, even if—and when—we make a few less-likely draws along the way. If we'd talked to just four people for that CBS News poll, no one would take that seriously. We might well have gotten two women and two men, but just one different pick would have given us a 3-to-1 split, quite far off from reality, and the margin of error would be so large we'd have no idea what the truth was. Draw samples in the hundreds, and the range starts shrinking, though not usually by enough. A margin of error on a sample of 100 is about 10 points, often still too wide to tell us something meaningful. But a margin of error on a sample of 500 is about 4 points. That is reasonable for some stories, and we can start to describe something we know about the world.

On a sample of 1,000, a poll will often report a margin of error of 3 points. If a poll reports an estimate of 50 percent with a margin of error of 3, we're saying we'd get values between 53 and 47 if we kept repeating the poll, and that the truth is in that range. That's often good enough for us to tell a meaningful story, such as how many movie fans there are. And we sometimes have to, because the margin doesn't get a lot better as we collect more samples from there. On a sample of 3,000 it's . . . about 2 points. We just tripled our sample size from 1,000 to 3,000 and barely dropped the margin of error. That's because there's always going to be at least *some* uncertainty arising from the fact that we haven't talked to everybody. Even if we drew huge samples of one million people, sometime along the way of drawing them pick by pick we'd get some samples that were 59 percent to 41 percent, or even 60-40, instead of being evenly balanced. Not many, but some. That's randomness at work, too. Samples, it turns out, work mathematically a lot like experience in life. Getting some is necessary, and getting a lot makes you good. But no matter how good you get, no one is perfect.

A sample of 1,000, which is often what major national polls use, is not magical so much as it is practical. Getting more information, perhaps by spending tons more money to pay interviewers, or spending six weeks gathering samples, won't get us better margins of error. We want enough information to think we're around the right answer and we recognize there will always be uncertainty.

As news pollsters, what we'd like to do, ideally, is have enough samples so that our margin of error is as meaningless to our story as aim was to Dirty Harry: as long as we are in range—and assuming we've done good sampling, we'll be quite sure we *are* in the range—then the interpretation of our results stays the same, no matter where in that range the truth actually lies.

The Margin Versus the Story

Consider this from a CBS News poll released in 2015: "The public continues to give Congress decidedly negative ratings. Only 15% of Americans approve of the job Congress is doing." Take into account the three-point margin of error for the poll, and it's still safe to say Americans don't approve. Maybe the right number is fourteen, or sixteen, but the margin of error doesn't change the story here. We know what we set out to learn either way. We didn't know if Congress was popular. We learned it is not. The margin of error often gets ignored in reports like this because it won't affect the story. The same would be true if the poll found that 90 percent liked Congress. Give or take a few points, Congress would still be fairly described as popular. (That's a hypothetical example, of course. We've never gotten a poll result with 90 percent liking Congress, which again shows you the reliability of sampling methods. And, perhaps, something about Congress.) Even if the finding were 51 percent approval, you still might then say, "Americans divide over their opinion of how Congress is doing" and be done with it.

But here's an example where a margin of error could matter in a story—not because of the sampling, but because of what we demand to know. Our CBS News national poll from August 2012, with a margin of error of three, said: "With the parties' conventions over and Election Day just weeks away, President Barack Obama has a three-point edge over Republican Mitt Romney among likely voters nationwide. Obama 49, Romney 46."

We've described Obama as having an "edge" in the poll. Because he has one. Yet if this were Election Night and the stakes were high as we reported this, it would not be entirely safe to call the race for Obama. The gap between him and Romney isn't big enough.

The margin of error applies to every number we report in a poll. It goes for both candidates. Just as we sought to find out how many movie fans *and* nonmovie fans there were, or how many men *and* women, we're finding out how many people favor Obama and how many favor Romney. Each candidate gets their own estimate.

In this case, if the margin of error is three points, that's putting the range three points to the high side for Obama—from his reported 49, up to 52 percent—and three points to the low side—from his reported 49 down to 46 percent. And for Romney, reported at 46, he gets the same margin of error applied, so that's a real value up as high as 49 and as low, perhaps, as 43. There's some overlap.

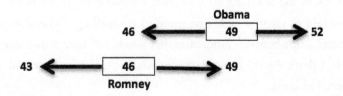

Obama probably does have more support than Romney. There's more room for possibilities given each of their ranges for that to be the case, and the numbers we report are in fact our best estimates for each candidate. There is a scenario, however unlikely, where Romney has more, where he is up at the top of his range at 49 and Obama is down at the bottom of his range at 46, and that what we're seeing is due to sampling error.

Suppose Obama was at 45 percent and Romney at 44 percent. A lot of times in cases like this, descriptions will call the contest "effectively tied," or even, or a "statistical tie." The better way, if less succinct or sexy, is to focus less on the race and more on the measure. Our best estimate is that Obama does have a one-point edge. And it is just harder to be sure that our best estimate is the case. To clear the margin of error for the difference between the candidates, to say that one really is leading, that gap needs to be about two times as big as the reported margin of error. It has to cover the highest the trailing candidate could be, and the lowest the leading candidate could be.

And most of the interesting races we're polling in are almost surely tighter than that, which is why they're of interest in the first place.

Margin of error calculations have no idea how the U.S. election system works; the math doesn't know that the leading candidate wins and the other goes home. If we must try to tell a story about a "leader," we've imposed that tension onto what we're looking at. Imagine if the context were different, if this were a proportional or parliamentary system where anyone getting over 20 percent, like both our example candidates are, would get some seats in the government. In that case we wouldn't care as much about the sampling error because we would know the story. Now the margin of error wouldn't be quite so compelling. Otherwise, we're imposing a line between candidates that would tell a particular story.

And that's the difference between what you can measure and what you need to know.

Chapter Eight

You Be the Judge

In the winter of 2017 the economy got a lot better, fast. Or so it seemed to a lot of people.

By some traditional measures, like the unemployment rate and stock market, things were about the same as they'd been for months. The unemployment rate was fairly low, as it had been. The stock market was up. The percentage of Americans who said the economy was "good" had begun to climb that fall, and now it really went up again. It rose six points in our poll just between December 2016 and February 2017, to the highest it had been since way back before the recession. And by the summer of 2017, those ratings would reach their highest levels in fifteen years. Was it rising because people were taking note of those measures— or was it something else?

Start with this: suppose you took a poll and were asked to rate the economy.

"How would you rate the condition of the national economy these days? Is it very good, fairly good, fairly bad, or very bad?"

How would you come up with an answer—meaning, before you think about what you *would* answer, ask yourself *how* you'd decide.

You might make an assessment of some kind by recalling that latest stock market index or that last unemployment stat you heard—what was that again?—or the jobs report or interest rates, or otherwise do your best to come up with something that gauges "the economy," whatever that is, which is sort of the point here. Maybe it's the assemblage of all those things. You'd cut yourself some slack, of course, knowing that few of us are actual economists, and even actual economists will disagree on which are the best measures to use for it all. All that would be a perfectly reasonable and objective way to think. You'd be trying to come up with a way to quantify something that doesn't inherently come with its own agreed-upon counter, which is basically tantamount to doing a bit of social science on the fly.

Then, when you see poll numbers from these items reported, you might expect your fellow Americans are using the same thought process to evaluate things. But that isn't what everyone does.

In January of 2017 Donald Trump took office, and that jump in economic ratings I mentioned came almost entirely from Republicans who suddenly decided the U.S. economy had gone from bad to good. The national rating would have been even bigger, too, if not for Democrats changing their evaluations in the other direction and more of them suddenly moved toward saying the economy was bad, though they didn't shift down as much as Republicans went up, so the net was still positive overall.

Back in December 2016, as the calendar had turned to winter and Barack Obama finished his term, a mere 31 percent of Republicans had called the national economy good. Trump was sworn in January 20, and in February, 61 percent of Republicans said it was good. By April, that had soared to 73 percent of Republicans, more than a 40-point jump for them from where it had been in a short time frame, all while those basic economic numbers like unemployment and the markets were not dramatically different. The poll question we've asked for decades, "How would you rate the condition of the national economy these days?," would seem to invite a neutral and objective evaluation of events beyond yourself, where you're evaluating how *things* are, not how *you* feel.

When we reported this, it seemed to some to be—somewhat dismissively—just a simple story about partisanship clouding the poll numbers and getting in the way of people's judgment. But it's really giving you a great insight into how people think about the world, which is just as interesting to a pollster as any number.

Over forty years of the CBS News poll, views of the economy have by and large moved with the times. Americans told us the economy was good during the mid-1980s economic boom, ratings fell in the recession of the early 1990s, then large majorities said things were "good" during the strong economy of the late 1990s; said things were okay during the early 2000s and ratings crashed—as in, fell-off-a-cliff crashed—along with the stock market at the end of 2008. By the winter of 2009 they hit 94 percent of people saying things were bad, an all-time low, and rose again slowly (very slowly) with the recovery afterward in the 2010s and on. In fact, the close connection between traditional economic measures and public views is the kind of big-picture finding that pollsters have long used to point out how well polling generally works. We do not see crazy polls with views saying "good economy" during recessions, and vice versa.

But amidst those sensible, general trends, there's something else going on: people whose party is *in* the White House consistently rate the economy higher than partisans of the party that's *out* of the White House. And this trend has gotten more pronounced.

In CBS News polls during George H. W. Bush's term in the late 1980s and early 1990s, Republicans rated the economy on average 19 points higher than Democrats did. There was a lot more partisan agreement during Bill Clinton's term, that gap was 6 points. In fact in almost 80 percent of the times the poll measured the economy during his term, and almost always after 1994, most Republicans at least said the economy was good. Heavy partisanship really kicks in during George W. Bush's time, with those eight years averaging a large 33-point gap in economic ratings, Democrats giving much lower ratings than Republicans. And just in terms of the dichotomous good-or-bad split, in most of the times we measured it most Republicans said the economy was "good" and most Democrats simultaneously said it was "bad." It wasn't until the 2008 downturn that they both agreed on something, that it had gone down to bad. Then we see a 25-point split, on average, between the parties during Barack Obama's term, with Republicans far below Democrats in their ratings. Democrats had returned to giving the economy "good" ratings after 2012 into Obama's second term—in fact eight in ten said it was good by the end—while most Republicans never did. They really only began to concur once the 2016 election was over.

Pollsters have been charting partisan splits like this in ostensibly objective evaluations for years. It's not just limited to the economy. It happens to a lot of "big" things people evaluate, the how-are-things-style questions, which shows there's a different decision-making process going on under the surface. It happens with war, too. Republicans decided the fight against ISIS went from going badly to going well, as soon as Donald Trump won. Democrats saw it heading the other way.

• • •

Before we judge our respondents for simply "being partisan" here, just what are the right answers to these questions, anyway? The topics we're asking about, like the economy, or progress in a war, actually are hard for regular people—and sometimes even for experts—to *quantify* in an objective way. There isn't one single, magic metric for what makes a "good" economy other than, maybe, the utopian condition that every single person is rich and happy, or as rich and happy as they ought to be, which of course doesn't happen. (And we ask how respondents are personally doing in a separate question, anyway.) Wars are hard to judge while they're going on and, even then, the longer-term implications, costs, and consequences are arguable to many people, at best. These are all complex ideas open to argument, and it's reasonable for different people to not just see it differently, but to evaluate it with different measures in the first place.

The partisan tinge to some of this comes, at least partly, from people who choose to use what we call shortcuts, or heuristics, to sort through complicated topics. These are simpler and faster ways for people to think—or at least to try to come up with an answer and a way of judging the world that makes sense to them. One easy shortcut is to just access whether you feel like your side, or your person, is running things. Having your party in power connotes there's someone steering in the direction you prefer. Many of us think any situation is better when we at least have a sense we've got some control over it. You might be driving in the pouring rain on awful roads, but you know you're a good driver, so "things," generally speaking, at least are better than they would be if you were in the passenger seat with a poor driver. Knowing whether your side is in charge also invites you, when you don't know an objective answer, to simply say what you want to be the case. Or partisans might simply be hearing messages and getting information—and interpretation—from their own party, which they've already decided is the source looking out for their interests.

Health Care

Sometimes people just admit they find a big, broad topic or a policy confusing, and that has real-world effects.

The health care law that passed in 2010 has gone by at least two names in wide use: the Affordable Care Act, and more colloquially—and politically—Obamacare. It's the same thing. A CNBC poll in 2013 asked half its respondents their feelings toward the Affordable Care Act and the other half their feelings toward Obamacare, replacing one name for the plan with the other for each group of survey takers. They got different answers. There was lower support of and more opposition to Obamacare, particularly from men and from Republicans, while young people and Democrats were more in favor of it.

Poll results like that are often held up as examples that how we ask questions matters a lot in what responses we get, which is true, but in this case we should go a step beyond to see what those different responses teach us about how people think and evaluate policies. The use of the name "Obama" in the term signals a political figure, of course, and for some that generates an emotional, reflexively positive reaction from those who like him, and a reflexively negative one from those who don't, or if you think you know which groups he favors and which he doesn't, a shortcut for whether the policy will be good for you or bad. For some people the political *is* how they evaluate complicated things, because it offers a quick way of decoding something that they're not otherwise very familiar with.

Shortcuts can be about "who gets what," which groups in particular will benefit and which might suffer, which is also often in debate when gauging forward-looking policies and is another way people evaluate them. If you've connected yourself to a party, you've probably already decided that party better represents the interests of people like you.

Pollsters make heavy use of these measures to describe why people might support a plan or not. Naming conventions aside, respondents did tell us they thought the new health law was perplexing. We asked straight-up as it was being debated and afterward, and most of the public declared that they thought Obamacare policy was confusing. (Which is also more evidence that people will admit to socially undesirable things in polls; here were a lot of them saying outright they were puzzled.) During the debate over the law in 2009, majorities of Americans in our polling said they didn't think President Obama had explained the plan clearly, either. When we asked people what they thought would happen once the plan went into effect, we got large numbers expressing skepticism, which is partially a fallback option people take when they face uncertainty about a change.

Into this vacuum steps partisanship. And we get polling divisions not merely because people are themselves partisan and want to echo their party, but because it helps them figure out whether this is good for them or not. If their partisan team thinks so, that's a signal. People chose the party in the first place because they felt it better matched the interests of people like them.

Support for the Affordable Care Act did rise over the course of time and reached a net positive in 2017, but many wanted changes, and polls still showed large partisan splits. Particular components of the law—such as the idea that insurance companies should be required to provide care for preexisting conditions—were extremely popular even as support for the law overall was split.

But larger values, too, underlie partisanship and still steer the way people judge policies on the issue. In recent polling Democrats and liberals have tended to say health care ought to be considered a right for all, whereas many conservatives and Republicans have tended to say it should be a product bought and sold in the marketplace like any other.

The Marriage Shift

In 2004 a CBS News poll release declared "Most Americans oppose gay marriage—and opposition appears to be increasing." Not so fast. Few viewpoints have changed as swiftly as those on same-sex marriage. That 2004 poll found 62 percent in opposition. By 2016 it was 62 percent in favor and rising, up from the year before. Evangelical Christians remained mostly opposed, and older Americans generally remained opposed more than younger ones.

Part of this shift is generational change, but in 2013 my colleagues Sarah Dutton and Jen De Pinto dug deeper and asked people if there had ever been a time when they'd been opposed. One-third said yes, they had changed their minds—which in itself isn't always something people admit or recall in polling. Asked in their own words why, the top answers respondents gave were that they knew someone personally who was gay.

Immigration

There are big age differences in views on immigration.

After the 1960s brought a round of widespread changes to immigration rules, "the foreign-born population quadrupled," according to a Census report, and the U.S. population went from having one in twenty people as foreign-born to one in eight by 2010. The Pew Research Center echoed that in the fifty-year span from 1965 to 2015, new immigrants and their direct family members (children and grandchildren) made up a majority of the U.S.'s total population growth. In *The Next America*, demographer Paul Taylor describes demographic transformation as "dramas in slow motion." So Americans of different ages start with very different contexts on the topic. The oldest cohort of today's

Americans, in particular those now in their retirement years, came of age in a workforce that was—numerically at least—far less impacted by that recent immigration than their younger counterparts. Today older voters also tend to be the most in favor of stiffer punishments toward those in the country illegally. Americans over age fifty are about twice as likely to favor a border wall as those under thirty. Americans under age thirty—a demographically diverse group themselves—have been the most likely to favor a path to legalization or citizenship for those in the U.S. illegally, and more likely to say immigration contributes to the nation.

Ron Brownstein, whose studies look at the nexus of demographic and economic transformation taking place, calls the demographic change "the most profound transformation since the Melting Pot era at the turn of the 20th century. . . . Among the young, the change is even more accelerated." Brownstein further notes that "even as these demographic and cultural shifts have rolled through American life, the economy has undergone an equally wrenching restructuring," pointing out that blue-collar, manufacturing, industrial jobs would account for only one-tenth of the professions that the Bureau of Labor and Statistics indicated would grow fastest by 2026, and made up far fewer of the jobs available today than they had in the 1960s. Instead, growth is coming in what Brownstein called "post-industrial" jobs like "health care, education, business services and tourism." In his work these factors are connected politically in what he calls coalitions of "transformation" and "restoration," between those who are comfortable with and advantaged by the shifts, and those longing for a return to a time, a generation or two past, before both those shifts occurred.

Polling on immigration also goes straight to ideas of a changing country and its connections to the wider world. It means trying to understand how people might be processing issues that range from job security, to cultural identity, to physical and national security, and even to the very definition of the country in the first place; of societal and economic change. Those ideas touch a lot more than particulars of policy like how many green cards get issued. And views on immigration get inextricably tied up with views about the immigrants themselves—who they are, what they do, and what they've done.

By 2015 Americans were twice as likely to say immigrants contributed to the country, as opposed to generally causing problems. That general sentiment in 2015 was nearly thirty points more favorable than it had been in the '80s and '90s. Familiarity has some role in how people answer this—as it does on so many attitudes—as more than half of Americans now report knowing someone or being related to someone who is an immigrant themselves. And in how the idea of immigration hews to national identity, to our collective sense of self, a Pew study in 2017 found two-thirds of Americans felt that "America's openness to people from all over the world is essential to who we are as a nation." There was another one-third who worried about things swinging too far in the other direction, that if America is "too open, we risk losing our identity as a nation."

People can hold different views of immigrants and their circumstances at the same time, and what Americans think about immigration policy of course depends heavily on what they believe immigrants do once they arrive. We tested some of this in 2018, asking Americans to describe illegal immigrants and offering a handful of descriptors, some with positive connotations, some negative ones. Two-thirds of Americans felt that illegal immigrants "fill jobs Americans won't do" and three-quarters described them generally as "hardworking people." Those two perceptions were linked: almost everyone who thought the former believed the latter. Two-thirds of Americans who felt immigrants were driving down wages also described those immigrants as hardworking.

This was also true of those urging the tougher measures against immigrants. Of people who said deportation of illegal immigrants should be the highest priority for the Trump administration, a majority 57 percent of them also called immigrants "hardworking people," so it wasn't simply that people opposed to immigration were going through the poll saying only negative things about them. A substantial eight in ten of these respondents also believed illegal immigrants drove down wages. Even among the most ardent backers of deportation, there was at least some perceived economic connection and rationale behind their views. They also expressed cultural concerns, too, more generally, that the rate at which the country was changing was occurring too fast, and were more likely to say immigrants made society worse.

Despite the attention drawn by the Trump campaign and the call for a wall along the Mexican border—which most Republicans supported and most Democrats opposed—immigration policies have actually divided the Republican Party for the last decade. In 2017, over half of Republicans were in favor of some kind of path to legal status or citizenship and fewer said immigrants should be required to leave. But Republican presidential primary voters, the people who choose the nominee that will face the wider electorate, were more in favor of stricter measures for those in the U.S. illegally than Republicans as a whole, and Donald Trump's voters, in particular, were especially high on such sentiment. In the 2016 primaries, voters were asked to pick their most important issue from a list. Immigration was not the top, paling in comparison to things like "the economy" that drew three and four times as much importance. But those who *did* pick immigration went for Donald Trump by overwhelming margins, by three- or four-to-one spreads in many states, not just border states. In Florida, Trump got 60 percent of voters who picked the issue of immigration as their top concern and his nearest competitor among those voters was Marco Rubio at 16 percent. In New Hampshire, Trump won most voters who felt, as a policy prescription, that illegal immigrants should be deported, and the nearest competitor got far fewer of those voters. The idea of a border wall showed differences between

Republicans generally and those who voted for Trump in the primaries. The latter were more supportive, almost entirely so.

That pattern continued into the Trump presidency. In our surveys in 2017 and 2018, the president's strongest backers, who tended to be older than other supporters, stood out in their opposition to immigration and paths to citizenship. They were strongest in their calls for deportation of illegal immigrants generally, and more of them opposed legal status for childhood arrivals even as the more conditional, softer Trump supporters—and the president himself—had said they favored it.

On that matter of DACA—Deferred Action for Childhood Arrivals—in particular, there was wide favor among Republicans for allowing some form of legalization or path to citizenship. Democrats agreed. And that underscored how differences over views of what immigrants had done, or not done, in entering the country was partially determining what the poll numbers were showing.

Nationally Democrats have more similarity across their ranks on the immigration issue but there are some small differences by race within the party. If we just look at white Democrats, two in ten feel illegal immigrants should be deported and two in ten say they drive down wages. Among African American Democrats, these numbers rise a bit to three in ten who want immigrants deported, and three in ten who say immigrants drive down wages; African American Democrats are the most likely to disagree with the idea that immigrants fill jobs Americans won't do. Possible economic stresses are more evident here when we look at income, as African American Democrats tend to have lower incomes than white Democrats, and so may be competing for some of the lower-wage jobs that they feel are being taken by immigrant labor. The same was true without controlling for race and just looking at lower-income and noncollege Democrats, a connection that suggests, even within partisan groups, they were at least partially looking at the issue through an economic lens.

Marijuana: An All-Time High

Back in 1979 a CBS News poll found just 27 percent of Americans thought marijuana ought to be legal. In April of 2017 a poll declared that support for general legalization had reached "a new . . . high" of 61 percent and nine in ten thought it at least should be legal for medical use. What changed?

There was clearly an example of generational shift. The baby boomers aged into their fifties and early sixties and were mostly supportive, as were those in their thirties and forties, and Americans under thirty-five voiced the greatest support of all at 76 percent. Only people over sixty-five were mostly opposed.

As recently as 1997 just a third of people said (and told pollsters) they had tried marijuana. Twenty years later half the country's adults said they had. People who've tried it are more likely to approve its being legal.

Drug use in general has undergone a change in perception in this regard: without specifying a drug, we simply asked how should habitual drug use be treated: as a criminal offense to be dealt with through the courts and criminal justice system, or as an addiction and substance-abuse problem, to be dealt with through the medical and mental health systems? A large 69 percent said it should be treated as a health and addiction issue. Once again there were distinct age differences, another sign that views on this are moving with the passing of generations and familiarity with the subject matter.

Things change. Poll numbers change. Sometimes because of what people do or do not know; and sometimes because of what people are—or aren't—familiar with.

Chapter Nine

It All Comes Down to Turnout

"Sometimes I think the whole system is bad."

"It wouldn't always change things."

We asked people who said they didn't always vote: why not? And those were among the top answers they picked, along with simply not being interested, or not having time.

Sometimes it doesn't even take an election to see the wide differences between people who engage with politics, and people who don't. In the spring of 2018, after a first year of the Trump administration that had dominated the daily news cycles and which was at turns tumultuous and historic, we asked people how they'd felt watching all the events unfold. Twenty-eight percent of Americans said the year had motivated them to get even more involved in politics. And more than a third said watching it all had made them just want to tune out.

For pundits the old line "It all comes down to turnout" is a throw-away phrase as Election Day nears—though not an incorrect one—meant to convey that we really aren't sure who'll show up to vote, and so we'll just wait and see; a bit of a way of hedging bets. For a lot of voters themselves, the very idea that someone wouldn't vote, or wouldn't be interested, can just seem baffling, drawing a sort of incredulous dismissal of "How can they think that way?" When we're polling elections we don't get those luxuries. We talk about voters, so we have to actually try to figure out just what it is that defines them. It's one of the hardest things we do. If you're a poll watcher, it's one of the biggest reasons you'll see differences in polls.

Only about 60 percent of Americans who can vote actually do, and that's in the very biggest, most attention-grabbing presidential elections where turnout hits its highest marks. In midterm Senate and congressional races only around 40 percent do, and that even dropped to a lowly 36 percent in 2014. In the primaries that pick the candidates in the first place, in special elections, and in local races, it dwindles even more. People can argue over whether that's healthy for a democracy. I can tell you it's a huge challenge for pollsters. If you thought it was tough taking a sample of the world, finding the people who'll vote means sorting through millions who won't.

This is not just a challenge for pollsters or a way for you to read the "likely voter" number in an election poll. It's a way of understanding the political outcomes that all of us see. People who vote are different from the population: they've historically been older, more partisan, and more intense about what they believe.

It might be the most impactful thing we uncover, and not just for our own poll numbers. Think about how much leverage over the world voters have over nonvoters. One way to see it is once that subset of voters divides in their choices—usually, fairly evenly between Democrats and Republicans—the winners' tallies look even smaller in comparison to everyone that could've shown up, let alone everyone they'll have to govern. Donald Trump's 63 million votes in 2016 and Barack Obama's 66 million in 2012, each of which sounds like a lot numerically, are each less than a third of everyone who was eligible to show up and potentially pick them. When Republicans won a House majority in 2014, their candidate totals represented less than one-fifth of potential voters. For the winners, that's a lot of leverage.

Why Vote?

Finding voters would be easier if it were exactly the same people who vote every election. There are a lot of repeat voters, but turnout varies enough that we won't be accurate if we try to poll the same people over and over. When we looked at the nation's voter rolls, we saw 26 million people who were old enough to vote in 2012 and didn't, but then *did* show up in 2016, while another 13 million traded places with them, sitting out 2016's contest after voting in 2012.

There's no single formula to the *way* some people decide whether to vote, or not, as it shifts with every campaign. One year some people might vote because they're drawn to the magnetism of a candidate. (In fact, when we asked people who had not shown up in 2016 why they hadn't, "I didn't like the candidates" was the second-most-selected answer, behind the top one: "just not interested.") The next election they might shrug but go to the polls out of a sense of civic duty. You won't find voters living in one special kind of place, either. Who votes in Minnesota? A lot of people. Minnesota routinely hits some of the highest marks for turnout in the nation at around 75 percent, along with places like New Hampshire, Maine, and Colorado. Big states like New York and California and Texas drop into the 50 percent range, but if you think it is large populations that make things lower, head out to Hawaii where turnout is the lowest in the nation, at just 43 percent. (It would be fun to just say folks there have other things to do. But it's probably that they don't often have very competitive elections; Democrats routinely win.)

So how do we find voters?

Actions and Words

We start with simple questions. We ask if you're registered, and that actually goes a long way. About eight in ten registered voters vote in presidential elections. Nonvoters tend to come from the ranks of people who are eligible to vote, in that they're old enough and citizens, but aren't registered to do so in the first place. Then we just ask if you're planning to vote, as in:

"How likely is it that you will vote in the election? Would you say you will definitely vote, probably vote, probably not vote, or definitely not vote in the election?"

The "definitely" people almost all do vote, as we learn when we check back with them or check the official vote records later. "Almost all," though, usually isn't good enough for us. We're trying to estimate contests just a point or two apart. And we know from years and years of polling—and as you saw in the 2016 case—that people tend to over-report their intentions. They aren't all outright lying, often they *mean* to vote, but things get in the way and their day gets hectic, or they realize they don't know where or how to, or they just plain lose interest. Some people don't think they will, but then a campaigner knocks on the door, or a friend persuades them, or some policy debate catches their attention and they decide to.

So a lot of pollsters add some other data into the mix, too, other things you tell us about yourself, other things we know about you, like how often you've voted before, or how much attention you're paying.

This is what we call a model, which combines multiple measurements of items that are linked to an action. This is no universal formula for what makes a voter vote, any more than a company can say with certainty who'll walk into their stores. Some folks call assembling this mixture of factors the "art" part of the polling job, and everyone I know does it a little differently. I once had an executive producer who used to drop in half-kidding references to Harry Potter and call it all the "dark arts," because some pollsters are notoriously secret about what's in their likely voter models—though I will share some of mine with you here. We've all spent years studying them, testing them, going back over what we did right and wrong, and so there is a little ego—and business success—involved in thinking we've come up with something great. Like most behavioral modeling, it is based on a pollster's decisions about what to include and how to mix the factors. And your poll will be off if, come Election Day, too many of your likely voters seem to have vanished.

The simplest of these approaches is when pollsters just take people who say they'll "definitely" or "probably" vote as "likely voters" and report that group. These polls tend to think of other modeling efforts the way I look at home repair projects, where the more tools you pull out to try to fix something just a wee bit better, the worse things actually end up. That's fair enough. My own view is that if you know something is for sure going to be incomplete, you've got to try to do a bit more.

Campaigns try to get your attention, and pollsters try to gauge your attention: *"How much attention have you been able to pay to the campaign—a lot, some, not much, or no attention so far?"* If you're interested in the first place, that's the first step to participating in something. You're reading about polling right now, so I'll assume you're interested in politics, and then I might assume you're a voter. That's an inference based on behavior.

And notice the construction of the question (which goes back decades) with that subtle but purposeful: ". . . have you *been able* to pay . . ." This feels like it takes a little of the pressure off, adding in that little tweak to be about ability, instead of just saying "How much attention do you pay?" It's not that you don't want to, this suggests, it's that circumstances might get in the way, like when you decline an invitation and say, "I can't make it, something came up." You'll see this in a lot of voting questions because we know voting is often viewed as a socially desirable thing, something you might believe we're all *supposed* to do. We want to avoid people saying they're paying more attention than they really are.

The Next Generation

Why haven't more young people voted in recent elections?

The Census reported that the 2016 turnout rate for people under thirty, while historically good for younger people, was still more than 24 percentage points lower than for people over sixty-five. Younger people, in particular, report being more skeptical that they have a voice in the process to begin with: in 2018 we surveyed a large sample of young adults under age twenty-four, and half of them felt that people their age had not much or no say at all in the political process; only one-third of adults over sixty-five felt the same. (Most young adults did feel their generation had an influence in popular culture.)

Yet there was a broader optimism, too: nine out of ten people under age thirty felt like their generation could change the world—or already was changing it. We found that more of them thought they could do that through supporting causes, rather than candidates. The Harvard Institute of Politics' long-running study of young voters led by pollster John Della Volpe finds them increasingly detached from the parties and the two-party system, and often favoring community service over campaigns as a means of involvement.

People vote when they think they have a stake in the outcome or in a community. If they live in one place for a long time, the chances that they vote might go up, because they either feel more connected to it or have time to see how politics affects things there. There have been years when the CBS News poll would ask how long have you lived at your current address with this idea in mind. If you own property, buy a home, or pay more property taxes, you're buying a stake in a place, too, and also now have more financial, material interest in things that are touched by public policy.

Younger people tend to be more mobile, with relatively fewer such attachments and less property, and that makes it harder to keep registration current, to say nothing of the fact that they just may have other things on their minds.

In our 2018 study, we asked people if they felt like part of a community, and nearly three-fourths of Americans who said they felt like they did also reported having voted in a recent presidential election or midterm; most said in fact that they "always" voted. Of those who said they did not feel like part of a community, only one-third reported always voting.

We also discovered, though, that it may matter less today whether that communal connection is physical or digital. Those who said the community they belonged to was "online" were just as likely to have voted as those who felt they were in physical communities like neighborhoods or towns.

It's Habit-Forming

Some pollsters try to figure out a lot without talking to people at all. Campaigns increasingly target voters using information like homeownership, or consumer and lifestyle data that might imply that people are passionate about a hobby or subject connected to policy (like the environment, guns, or investing). This may affect not only a poll that you see. If you get a piece of mail about a campaign or a knock on your door, and wonder why they sent it to you or came to your house—or even more precisely, to you but not your spouse—some data firm may have targeted you based just on this kind of information even if you've never answered a survey. The gun owner might be assumed to be a Republican—rightly or wrongly—and the donor to environmental causes might be assumed to be a Democrat, and if passionate about those policies, more liable to be a voter.

Whatever the model, I think talking to people can always help. Take me as an example. There are a lot of things I could go to—or "turn out" for—in New York, such as professional sporting events and concerts. If you saw that I read hockey magazines or downloaded songs you would rightly conclude I like sports and music, but then why don't I ever buy tickets and "turn out" for hockey games or concerts? I don't have time to go. If you asked me that, I'd tell you. Voting, too, takes resources, and one of them is time.

Then every year you hear about "enthusiasm" for a candidate, a campaign, the crowds, the volunteers. So we could ask: *"Thinking about the . . . election, overall, would you say you are very enthusiastic, somewhat enthusiastic, not too enthusiastic, or not enthusiastic at all about voting?"* But the trouble with relying too much on the enthusiasm measure is that a lot of people just see voting as a duty, and excitement or enthusiasm has nothing to do with it. Motivation might apply differently to a young voter who's never voted before and needs an extra push to come out, while someone who's done it dozens of times does not. We do see turnout go up when a race is competitive and people feel they can make a difference.

In our 2018 study, after a string of special elections (like the one in Alabama) in which Democrats had seen high turnout, eight in ten

Democrats said watching those races had made them feel more motivated to help the party as the midterm races began. And two-thirds of Republicans said those special elections had motivated them, too: to get out and oppose the Democrats.

And sometimes a person just has to be asked by the eager campaign worker or, even better, neighbor or friend, who knocks on your door or calls to tell you about the election and a candidate can remind people to vote, or point them to the right place to register or help them do it. So we ask people: *"Have you been personally contacted by either one of the presidential campaigns?"*

If you're like me, you probably get catalogues in the mail from the retailers you already ordered from. (I really need to get off those mailing lists.) And I keep seeing pop-up ads for sneakers that I already bought—and still haven't worn out—which means someone somewhere thinks I am a sneaker buyer. That's true. Just about everywhere you turn, some marketer or advertiser figures that your past actions can define you. That's true in voting. People who vote tend to "be" voters, which is to say they keep on doing it, at least in the big elections, and pollsters lean on the idea. Here's how:

Elections officials record whether we vote or not in each election and that information is by and large publicly available. (They don't record who you voted for, that's a secret, of course.) They might also record the method you used, absentee, or early, or in person at the polling place, which is also useful to know. Private companies like L²Systems, whose data we use at CBS News, cull this information and assemble it into databases and files that campaigns or pollsters like us can analyze.

Suppose I go through the voter records, and take currently eligible people who've voted in the last presidential election four years ago *and* then voted in the midterm two years *after that*, and see that almost all of them—more than 96 percent—also voted a third straight time, in the following presidential election, too. So people who voted in 2012 and 2014 almost all showed up in 2016, which means that had I polled them, I wouldn't have really even needed to ask them what they intended to do that year. I could instead have just assumed they'd show up, based on that past behavior, and I would have been right 96 percent of the time.

People with strong voting histories might count for more in a poll's "likely voter" assessment than people who seem wishy-washy about the prospect of voting. To turn that likely voter assessment into a single number, we give everybody a score, assembled from how they rate on any or all of factors like those I've described, expressed intention, motivation, history. One means I think you're a certain voter. Zero means you are not.

Voting history goes into the score. In our example, any respondent in the poll who has that regular profile of past voting might get a score of .96 on that scale of 0 to 1, reflecting that real-world finding that it is 96 percent of habitual voters who turn out. As in a lot of social science, we're making an inference about an individual based on the characteristics of the group they belong to. If our respondent then tells me they intend to vote, or already have by absentee ballot, their score might go up even more.

Then again, I might give a lower score to people who voted only in a past presidential election but not a past midterm. This is a person who doesn't vote every time; on the voter files, they turn out less frequently. I might also give a score to respondents based on attention (people paying more get a higher score than people paying less), based on what we've seen high-attention people do in the past.

When we combine everyone in the poll to give you a percentage for "likely voters," these scores are used as what we call likely voter *weights*, or the relative amount of influence given to each particular person in the sample. Everyone is made to represent what we believe to be their true share of the likely voter population, based on their own characteristics. Translated to real life, and taken as a whole, this part of the poll sample should represent the part of the population that really does show up to vote.

What's the World Supposed to Look Like, Anyway?

Which brings up the debate over what the electorate ought to look like, once you've identified its voters. This is where you start to see people argue about "who the poll talked to" or the idea that it "talked to too many" of one group or another. Sometimes it's an argument over demographics: what the percentage of white or black or Hispanic voters there ought to be in a poll; or men and women of various education levels. All of those variables are determined in large part by what the pollster believes the likely electorate will look like, especially when the poll is a sample of likely voters instead of all Americans; who among those groups they believe is a voter, and who isn't. Very often the argument uses an even simpler metric: whether a poll has, supposedly, "too many" Democrats or "too many" Republicans.

The first answer to this usually comes from looking at actual turnout. While Americans overall *call* themselves independent or Democrat at a higher rate than call themselves Republican, Republicans have shown up to vote at relatively higher rates. So polls of all Americans usually have more Democrats in them because that's what's out there, but polls of voters (with likely voter models) often get closer to an even balance between the parties.

For example, all Americans in 2016 in CBS polls said they were: 26 percent Republican, 42 percent independent, 31 percent Democrat.

But *voters* in 2016 said they were: 33 percent Republican (that's

7 points higher than the population); 31 percent independent (11 points lower than Americans as a whole); and 36 percent Democrat (5 points higher than all Americans).

In recent years this has been especially true in the midterm elections, like 2014, which was a lot more Republican than the adult population as a whole. Republicans even straight outnumbered Democrats at the polls that year. On Election Day, the number of independents goes down, relative to the whole. And younger people have stayed home in relatively far greater numbers, at least in recent years.

What if people switch parties? The fact is—and the good news for pollsters trying to get the right numbers—people don't switch very often, from what we've seen over the years, and when they do switch it happens very slowly, and then they tend to call themselves independents. The number of self-identified independents in America is on the rise, though glacially. In CBS News polls from the late 1970s on through the early 2000s, we saw independents, Democrats, and Republicans staying in roughly the same relative proportions. That's generally the tale until around 2010, as the independent label starts to rise and the partisans begin to drop. Then as the 2010s progress, the percentage saying they're independent climbs up from the 30s into the low to mid 40s by 2018.

But if you're polling a campaign, over a few months or a year, you can expect to see partisanship hold steady. We tested this in 2017 with our CBS News Nation Tracker surveys. That set of polls—in polling terms a panel study—was designed to keep reinterviewing the same representative sample of people, every month or two, to see if their attitudes changed on the issues facing the country, and then if they had changed, to let them explain why. My colleagues and I looked at partisanship among our respondents over the course of the year. We had interviewed them up to five times from January to July. People stuck with their parties: 91 percent of respondents told us they were still with the same party in the summer as they had been the first time we asked them about it that winter. Most of the movement was confined to people switching in and out of the independent category, flirting with a major party and then moving back to independent. It was very rare to see someone identify as a Democrat and then say they were a Republican in some later month, and vice versa. Just 3 percent of people who were initially Republicans became Democrats, and just 2 percent of initial Democrats went the other way to become Republicans.

The people who did move were younger, perhaps not yet having formed a strong partisan attachment, and less attentive to politics overall.

Just How Independent?

No one gets through an election season without hearing a pundit or two talk of how independents will swing an election. This is simply not always the case. (Just ask Mitt Romney, who won independents when he ran for president in 2012.) That's partly because "independent" is a bit too broad a label. There are different kinds, and not all are the kind of savvy, weigh-the-options-and-then-decide swing voters that their name suggests. People who pay less attention to politics overall are more likely to call themselves independent. And people who are disaffected and fed up with the whole system often call themselves independent.

Many independents look a lot like partisans by another name. They might be picking the term "independent" because it conveys a sense of being a thinker as opposed to being a follower. In 2016, half of all independents who went to the polls had a favorable view of only one of the parties, but not both. Twenty-three percent of independents had a favorable view of only the Republican Party, and 27 percent saw only the Democratic Party favorably. That's not exactly a profile of voters considering both sides.

When we've asked independents to describe who they *usually* vote for, almost half of them said they picked a single party more often than not. There are effectively Republican independents—23 percent said they always or usually voted for Republicans—and Democratic ones, 21 percent reported always or usually voting for Democrats. In both cases there were more who said "usually" than "always." That once-in-a-while difference, however infrequent it was, can also confer a feeling of being independent. Forty percent of independents report themselves as voting "equally for both" Republicans and Democrats over recent elections.

There are hints this may start changing. Younger people *are* more independent, and studies suggest millennials and the generation behind them as remaining distant from both parties. A Pew Research Center report in the spring of 2018 traced the voting history of millennials (born between 1981 and 1996) and showed that while the Democrats had an advantage over Republicans among them, millennials were "more likely than those in older generations to call themselves independents." Pollster Kristen Soltis Anderson finds millennials are not following the old models of how people pick a party as they get older.

This is one reason the campaigns today often try to stress get-out-the-vote efforts to get their loyal supporters to the polls as much as, or even more than, trying to persuade swing voters to change positions. They're just responding to what voters regularly do—and what nonvoters don't.

Chapter Ten

Counting on Congress

Jane from Arkansas was kind enough to answer our national poll in 2014 and said she was planning to vote for a Democrat for Congress. We counted her in the poll, but I know that when Election Day rolled around, she didn't.

She wasn't lying. She just never got the chance. Don't worry, nothing happened to Jane. It's just that her district is so lopsidedly Republican that the Democrats didn't even field a candidate that year.

Stan was from Maryland, and he took the poll, too. He said he was paying attention to the election, and that he always voted, and was voting for a Democrat. We recorded his choice, and with Stan, I'm sure he did actually vote for one. But the Democrats were going to win his district no matter what Stan did. They do all the time, with at least 70 percent, and did again that year.

It might feel like Jane's and Stan's stories should be unusual, ones I've cherry-picked from places that are lopsided and partisan. In fact, I picked them because they are examples of *most* people's situations.

Tune in on Election Night to see who controls the majority in the House of Representatives, with 435 races going on from every corner of the country, and you'll be watching an election where the overall winner hinges on what happens in a relatively small group of districts and the rest are all but foregone conclusions. At our House section at the Decision Desk, where we'll call all 435 races, we'll know that only a relative few seats will be competitive, depending on the year, and even in a potentially tumultuous year.

Looking back through our records from the Desk, on average for the last four election cycles, fewer than one in ten voters has lived in a congressional district where it seemed to us that *either* party had a shot at winning the seat heading into Election Day. The other nine in ten voters were more like Stan or Jane, living in districts where the outcomes were predictable, even if they were contested. The typical congressional race is won with more than 60 percent of the vote—not close. This has big implications for how we measure it all, and how to read the congressional polls leading up to Election Day.

Does It Matter if They're Unpopular?

Congress has plumbed the depths of unpopularity in recent years. Congress's approval rating hovered around 15 to 20 percent approval for a while. In the 1990s it wasn't unusual to find congressional approval in the 40-percent range at times, which is not great, but not awful either. The most recent spate of rock-bottom ratings were during the recession and the economic crash—which may also say something about Congress's response to that crash. The specific complaint, Americans say, is that Congress is too partisan and doesn't get enough done because of that.

Even among House seats that are competitive, not all actually change hands from one party to another in any given year. In 2016, the Democrats gained 6 seats across 435 contests. In 2014, 13 more seats went to the Republicans out of 435. Some larger gains have seen Democrats net 31 and 21 seats across two cycles (2006 and 2008, respectively), and Republicans get 63 seats in 2010 alone. We looked at the contests going back to 2002, for almost 3,000 House elections held in total, and a mere 6 percent of contests have seen a party turnover from Democrat to Republican, or Republican to Democrat, in that time frame.

More than 90 percent of incumbent candidates who run are reelected, each and every year, but even without them running, districts tend to stay in the same party's hands. One of the more durable sayings you'll hear from pundits is that Americans dislike Congress but like their own representative. That's not quite the way to put it, I think. There is one thing they like about them, in particular.

It's not clear everyone knows their congressman by name. A Gallup poll in 2013 found that only one-third could name theirs. (On the other hand, one can argue over what it means to know, or remember: it's hard to recall a name out of the blue when the pollster calls, but you might remember it when you see it on the ballot, or in an ad, like the way you can't remember that so-and-so actor but you know his work, and when you see his TV show again the name pops into your head.)

But more Americans do seem to know the *party* of their representative—in particular, those who are more engaged and more likely to vote are more apt to know their congressperson's party. We asked people in a 2018 poll whether they were represented by a Democrat or a

Republican, or were not sure. (We knew which districts the respondents lived in, but didn't say so when we gave them the poll.) Fifty-four percent could respond correctly, after accounting for the one-third who outright told us they weren't sure. It did not look like guessing: the more politically engaged were more likely to know, and voters got it right more than nonvoters. Seventy-three percent of all partisan voters, those who affiliated themselves with a party, got it right. The more ideological they were, the more likely they were to be correct. Very conservative Republicans who offered an answer, for instance, were almost entirely likely to know when they were represented by a Republican, and to a greater extent than their moderate counterparts were.

Whether they know them or not, it's hardly clear everyone actually likes their representative. That doesn't mean they don't vote for them anyway.

In the fall of 2014 in our polling, only 32 percent of voters said their *own* member of Congress deserved reelection. In those pre-election polls, in districts that were represented by Republicans, half of Republican voters said their own Republican representative did not deserve reelection. But then asked whether they were *voting* for "the Republican," nine in ten Republicans said yes.

Meanwhile, Democrats living in Democratic-held districts were almost as skeptical of their own representative, with over four in ten saying he or she didn't deserve reelection; and once again, nine in ten said they were voting for "the Democrat" anyway.

Then exit polls showed they did exactly that when Election Day came around. Ninety-four percent of incumbents who sought reelection won it. Maybe "deserve" has nothing to do with it: they may not like him or her, but they do seem to like the party he or she belongs to.

Being Predictable

So for many voters, it's the party that matters. And increasingly so. House voters are sticking more and more to their party over time, just like their representatives are sticking more and more to theirs once they get to Washington. In the 1980s about 20 percent of Republicans voted Democratic in House contests, and almost as many Democrats crossed back the other way. By the early 1990s crossover starts to decline, and these days crossover has dropped like the temperature in a polar vortex, down into the low single digits: just 4 percent of Republicans voted for a Democrat in the House in 2016, and only 7 percent of Democrats crossed.

When an incumbent steps aside, partisan patterns still hold plenty of sway. Our analysis of recent races showed that when an incumbent has decided not to run, the opposing party has gained about seven points from how they did before. So a Republican retiring will often be replaced by a new Republican representative; a Democrat giving up a seat will be succeeded by another Democrat, with an election that looks fairly similar to the one before it.

With all that partisanship, the better way to describe congressional voting may not be so much that voters like their congressperson. It's more that partisans in a district really, really like their congressperson's *party*.

When congressional districts are gerrymandered, they're mapped with partisan intent, so that the balance of voters in them favors one party over the other. From a pollster's point of view, what we see is so many voters behaving in a consistently predictable, partisan manner that it's surely easier for those who would try to gerrymander to do so. If someone wants to ensure that a district will go for one party or the other, predictable voters are easier to draw lines around.

Don't Be Generic

In the run-up to a congressional election, if you want to know whether the House majority might flip or not, look at the districts that have competitive races going on in them. Looking at national polls won't tell the whole story. National polls report a *national* preference for Congress—what's called the "generic ballot"—which simply asks people nationwide if they'd prefer "the Democrat" or "the Republican." You'll see this poll number reported as "Democrats have a six-point lead in the Generic Ballot, 53 to 47," or so, and many pollsters put out the number in part because it just makes it easier to have one question that everyone in the country answers. This raises a Stan-and-Jane problem. There are 435 separate races going on, and most of them are not really in danger of changing party hands, even in a big "wave" year, and certainly not in a conventional year. But the national polls are including everyone, among them a lot of people like Stan and Jane—people whose votes aren't really going to swing control of Congress, because they live in districts that are safe for one party or the other. That's a lot of useless information baked into the poll numbers: they could include shifts such as Democratic districts going from, say, 60 percent Democratic to 70 percent Democratic. That *won't* change who wins those seats and it *won't* decide who controls Congress, but it *will* make the national poll numbers twitch. The national poll has all the Stans and Janes.

Nor is there is a particular percentage of the national vote that automatically gives a party control of the House. In fact, the percentage of seats that a party wins isn't the same as the percentage of national vote it gets. Democrats actually won a majority 51 percent of total House votes in 2012 and did not win a majority of seats, instead they won 46 percent of seats. Democrats won 47 percent of all votes in 2014 and 43 percent of seats. Partly as a result of geography—they tend to live in densely populated urban areas—and partly as a result of gerrymandering, Democrats tend to be more concentrated in fewer districts. So running up national margins doesn't always equate to flipping seats.

It's like in baseball's 2016 World Series, when the Indians and Cubs scored the same amount of total runs in the seven-game series, but the Cubs won more games, and games are what count. Think of runs like votes and districts like games. Or more politically analogous, like the Electoral College, where candidates can win the national popular vote and lose the Electoral College by racking up big wins in some states while losing a lot of others narrowly.

Watch the *list* of competitive House races in the fall of an election year. And just follow any polls that only concentrate in competitive districts alone, or look at specific House-seat-estimate models that offer a sense of how many specific seats are liable to flip, instead of just a national percentage. If the number of seats "in play," or which are rated as highly competitive, gets big, then chances are control of the House majority is up for grabs.

As a rule of thumb, a gauge I use is whether the number of very competitive districts is twice the gap separating the parties in the House. For example, in the spring of 2018, we saw about fifty competitive races, with more on the radar that might become competitive later, and the Democrats needed half that to take the House. So at the time we said House control could be in play.

That's because not all the competitive contests flip; partisanship still has a strong pull.

Then on Election Night, we can often call House control by looking for patterns across similar districts as polls close east to west. If, for example, Republicans are winning their races easily on the East Coast, we can infer something about how similar districts are going in the Midwest and on the West Coast; the Republicans might win them, too. Districts become data points, like counties do and precincts do. If the Democrats are winning seats early, with a consistent gain in each, we can apply that gain to other districts that haven't counted all their votes yet, and estimate what is happening elsewhere before all the vote reports are in.

If partisanship is a big factor, the other is the president. In midterm years, the president is "on the ballot" even though he isn't running. In the spring of 2018, our polling showed an even split between those who planned to cast a midterm vote in support of President Trump and those who planned to oppose him, but in either case, more than two-thirds called him a factor in their planned vote. Historically, that would not surprise. A majority of voters in the three midterms 2006, 2010, and 2014 all said that their vote for Congress was meant to either support or oppose the sitting president's agenda. Historically a first-term president's party has usually—but not always—lost seats in the midterm. Not every year fits the pattern. In 2002, in the wake of the 9/11 attacks and the strong approval of his handling of it, President George W. Bush was able to buck that trend. But in 2006, Bush's second midterm with the Iraq War increasingly unpopular, more voters said their vote was to oppose him than to support him, and Democrats regained the majority in the House. In 2010, President Barack Obama's first midterm as president, more said their vote was to oppose his policies than to support them, and the Republicans took the House.

Chapter Eleven

Is It Really a Horse Race?

This is a story about President Jeb and a bottle of wine.

I'm not a wine connoisseur. I like beer. So if I do have to buy a bottle of wine, I look at the prices and I assume the expensive ones taste better than the cheap ones and I pick the priciest one I can afford. I do that because I think a number—in this case, the price—tells me a story. I imagine what led to it, back-filling facts I do not have. The quality of grapes must have been higher, because those cost more, the barrel must have taken weeks to craft, and that labor cost was passed along, which led to the high price in front of me. It's a decision-making shortcut economists have long known that we use, and that the marketers know can fool us.

We do this with all kinds of numbers we see, though, spinning stories from a digit, certainly with those that represent results or tallies. The kid got a 1600 score on her SAT tests, so she's smart. Or maybe she just memorized how to take the test. We just check the score and the Dallas Cowboys won the game. Did the quarterback play well, or get hurt? Looking for shortcuts like this might at first sound like a simplistic or even a lazy thing, but it can actually be quite rational over the long term; rational in that sense of gaining a lot of knowledge from just a little bit of learning, from seeing one thing that we think describes everything. We take the smaller amount for the sake of efficiency, make inferences from it, and move on.

As it turns out, blind taste tests show that when people don't know the prices, many actually like cheaper wines better.

Like me staring blankly at a wall of wine bottles in a liquor store, a lot of folks are inundated with polls and numbers these days, and it can be hard to sort through all the products. There are polls and there are poll averages and aggregators and forecasters, and you've got a lot to choose from. It may even sound odd I'm listing them out as different, they're so conflated in the public mind as just simply "the polls," and all of us as "pollsters." How you deal with it all depends on what you need to know.

Before an election, poll numbers that show vote choice, the ones that say who's "winning," can easily tempt us into using that shortcut as we follow the campaign. Candidate Smith 45, Johnson 42. They look like scores. They're treated like scores. In fact, the moniker for this is "the horse race." Around the newsroom we can ask for a graphic to be shown on television just that way: order up the "horse race" graphic from the control room.

If we see that a candidate is leading, it can feel like we know a larger story: that the last big speech the candidate gave found favor, or that his tax plan is popular, or that lots of people approve of him personally, or any number of other inferences, the way I made up a story about what led to the price of the wine. Pollsters have a long history of trying to get people, including the news media, to ease off the use of this vote choice, especially for setting context, which can make it seem like it has more explanatory power than it does. "Trailing in the polls," a report might begin, implying to the audience that whatever the candidate is doing today is some kind of desperate catch-up ploy, for example, when it's really just a speech about tax policy that the candidate has been crafting for months.

Jeb Bush was the top name in some vote-choice polls for the Republican nomination in 2014, more than a year before the 2016 primary contests actually began. He also topped the list of candidates we gave people and asked whom they'd even consider voting for. Jeb Bush wasn't "leading" that race. There was no race, really. All those horse race polls were telling you was that Jeb Bush's name—owing to his famous father and sibling who were presidents—was the best known, so poll respondents were just picking it out because they recognized it in a long list of other, unknown people, like Bobby Jindal or Ben Carson. Pollsters call this a function of "name ID."

It certainly didn't tell you Jeb was running a strong campaign or that Republicans would actually vote for him to be president—as he quickly learned when the primaries did start.

Even in the heat of campaigns, the vote choice leaves out critical information. In the summer of 2004 John Kerry had a lead on George W. Bush when we asked people who they were voting for. Did voters therefore think Kerry would make the right decisions in Iraq, with the war raging, or in an international crisis more broadly? We asked that, too, and, no they didn't. That ultimately mattered more in voters' final decision making.

Importantly, this is different from the polls being "wrong" or statistically off. The numbers might be accurate at the time, in the sense that they properly reflect the public's answers to a question that was put to them. It is a different kind of error. We risk inferring too much by reasoning from this simple political scoreboard, and we can miss the really important story—the one that would have made us discount that number, not because of any computational accuracy, but because of the real story hiding behind it. Or put another way, as when I talk about this around the newsroom and I find myself sounding like Inigo Montoya, the swordsman in *The Princess Bride* who's become an Internet meme, "I do not think it means what you think it means."

While Hillary Clinton was leading Donald Trump, voters also held very unfavorable views of her personally at the same time. She had the lowest favorability rating of any front-runner we'd measured. But it might have been readily assumed from her lead—as some observers and perhaps her own campaign did—that those ratings didn't *matter* because Donald Trump was also viewed so negatively. That was wrong and you needed a battery of interview questions to see it. People with a negative view of both candidates were not as firm in their candidate choice— though they did have one—as people with a positive view of at least one of them. Twenty percent of the Clinton voters with a negative view of *both* her and Trump also said they'd consider switching their vote to Trump, a higher rate than others, and people with negative views of both were three times more likely to have waited until the last few days before the election to decide—they might not have shown up in the head-to-head horse race, at all. And we know from the exit polls the late deciders went for Trump.

Instability was a better, more insightful story in the sense that it more accurately described the contest. If you knew those factors you didn't yet see in the horse race and could not have gleaned from the horse race numbers alone, you might have known something bigger was going on under the surface. The horse race was measuring something it never had before—a race where both candidates were disliked—so its context could not be compared to the past as easily. The horse race "results" meant less than they usually did.

Is More Always More?

Even the metaphor of a horse race itself is inapt. The horses cover a specific distance and the times they post belong to them forever, never to be taken away no matter who wins. People's opinions aren't given over to anyone forever. If candidate Jones, heretofore leading in every poll 55–45, suddenly says something really stupid, he could lose in a 99–1 landslide—and he doesn't get to keep that 55 percent he had in the polls.

There are, though, more vote-choice (or horse race) poll numbers out there than ever. Long-distance dialing got cheap, voter lists helped make dialing more efficient, online interviewing became common, media coverage demanded them, and we've seen more and more polls because of it all. This is a good thing. People have incentive to do them because they're popular. Private firms found that doing polls was a good way to get their names out in public. Colleges did, too. Places like Quinnipiac University, a small Connecticut school that made an investment in a prolific polling center, got their name on the news, and raised their profile with it so much that the school became nationally known and saw a rise in applications. Polling is hard, but it's a lot easier than getting a basketball team to the Final Four.

A quick count at the website RealClearPolitics.com's listing from May to November 2016 showed more than 250 national horse race polls were publicly released for the general election alone, dozens more from myriad battleground states, and not counting all the primaries that came earlier that spring or the various other Senate or congressional contests. Another study put the total number of public polls of any sort well into the thousands. In 2012, pollster Mark Blumenthal notes, his website Huffpost Pollster "logged 1,240 state-level polls that asked an Obama-Romney trial heat," testing a matchup between the two.

All of them can feel like news, even if they aren't. Walk through our

CBS newsrooms on any given day during the height of the campaign, and you'd see dozens of producers and broadcast associates monitoring mailing lists and a steady stream of newswire items: poll release after poll release is getting sent in to us. Pick any stretch of time: over the course of three days in late October there were eight national horserace estimates from reputable organizations reported. And that's not counting the ones focused on specific states—a couple from Florida, a couple from Colorado or Ohio—on any given day. It's all good, that is, unless we pay too much mind to just that horse race part.

Along with the increase in polls and that insatiable demand, the horse race aggregator websites have boomed. They combine vote-choice numbers taken from various polls. These aggregator websites draw millions and millions of page views; you've probably seen them, and maybe even check in regularly. There's RealClear Politics, which compiles just about every poll from every race as far as I can tell. Huffpost Pollster, which was formerly Pollster.com. Best known is probably *FiveThirtyEight* from Nate Silver (which aggregates current polls but also makes forecasts about the future, and the latter is something different again). *The New York Times* covers data journalism broadly with the "Upshot" section. Prominent on many of these pages—and above what are usually interesting analyses— you see a big, single-digit summary of all the latest percentages pollsters have put out for each campaign's horse race number. It might include our CBS News poll, and Quinnipiac University's poll, and NBC's, and CNN's, and the *Washington Post*/ABC News poll, and so on and so on, some well-known and some not, all boiled down together and distilled in some fashion into one blue Democrat number and one big Republican number. It is the horse race, on steroids.

Mark Blumenthal started Mystery Pollster in September of 2004 and Pollster.com in 2006 along with Charles Franklin, adding poll averages in chart form; Blumenthal has also written on the history of poll aggregation. His study of the subject notes the appearance of combined averages as early as *The Economist's* "poll of polls" as far back as 1992, and Bill Schneider's "poll of polls" combinations of polls for CNN in 1996, all aimed at seeing—Blumenthal's study quoting Schneider— "how much consistency there is across all the polls." The impetus behind all this being that "at its best, poll aggregation can make sense of a deluge of polling data. . . . An average of competing polls illustrates the range of random error and puts the results of a single poll sponsored by a news organization into broader context." To you at home, that context is: if CBS, or another organization, releases a horse race poll that's different from many others, you the consumer might want to know that it is different—whether or not it is *right*, of course, is another matter. Blumenthal's study counted the Google searches for the word "poll" over ten years and showed "massive spikes of 10 to 20 times baseline search volume just before the general elections of 2004, 2008 and 2012" and describes the pattern: "Like baseball fans checking the standings, these political enthusiasts never tire of checking the latest polls to see how their 'team' is doing and whether it is on track to win the big prize."

Polls Are Not a Poll

All of that is fun. But despite the shared nomenclature, these aggregations are not "polls." Aggregations are to polling what a DJ's nightclub playlist, mixing rhythms of various songs, is to a songwriter: good for times when the audience wants to hear the beat, but not listen to the music. A poll— a survey—talks to people like you. An aggregation of horse races does not. Each good survey asks for people's motivations and considerations behind the vote choice it is measuring, and every pollster approaches that attempt at understanding a little differently in the questions they ask and how they analyze the answers they receive. A survey shows you *why* people are voting as they are, not just *that* they're voting as they are.

To the poll watcher, an aggregation is a secondary source in two respects: it's derived from others' polls, and an aggregation hasn't directly interviewed anyone in putting together its numbers. So it cannot in itself directly explain anyone's thinking. It cannot tell the story inside the numbers, the way we could when we looked more closely at the kinds of people voting for Clinton or Bush or Kerry or Trump.

The point of a poll is not only to count, but also to interview and understand people. So in the newsroom what I recommend we report, wherever possible, is the same advice I'd give you outside it. Find out what's going on by picking one good poll and reading it—a specific poll that *explains* the race. Ask which survey advances the *story*, not just the score. Do we have convincing evidence in a new poll that, say, candidate Jones's big economy speech has fallen flat? Do we know that that's reflected in the horse race, by seeing people who hated the speech also say they're now less inclined to vote for Jones? Or did the poll even ask about that? Is it a surge among young voters for candidate Smith now propelling her into the lead, and if so, *why*? Do they say they love her college savings plan? Hopefully the poll asked about the college savings plan. If so, okay, that's an explanation. Or else, is this just another election poll within the margin of error?

We pollsters do have to reckon with why people want the shortcut in the first place. America has very long campaigns, among the longest in the world, and they are winding narratives full of personalities and policies and arguments, so it's alluring to find something to do for the election contest that what (we think) the price tag and the sports score do for summarizing the value of products or what happened in a game. If you really, really need to know who's leading—not going to win, mind you, *leading*—the aggregations are a fine way to know, at least later in the campaign. But that is the only question, albeit an important one, that a single number really tells you. If you want to explain why the race moved, or why a poll got what it got, then it's only a number. That goes for whether it is derived from one hundred horse races or a single horse race. It's the same as me checking that tag on the bottle of wine: a shortcut, often good enough to backfill an explanation, but one that also leaves us highly susceptible to an error—the error of missing the better story.

At the Scene . . .

As a news pollster I've been taught to see a poll as a report like any other you'll see on our broadcasts: it should be our best information of what's going on, for which we're uniquely responsible. When our poll gets merged with pollsters' work in an aggregation, it's now involved in something different. I've used the following example talking to our producers.

A reporter gets to the scene of a bank robbery that just happened downtown. The robber has fled and the cops are scouring the place. The reporter interviews a detective who tells her that witnesses described the robber as really tall, six foot six. She talks to a second detective who says other witnesses, over by the door, described a guy really short, five foot two. Should she get her microphone, go on TV, and say, "Police are looking for a robber who's medium height, five foot ten?" No.

Instead, she could go talk to witnesses herself and see which had the better vantage point, find out how those detectives came by their information, and pick one. Maybe one witness was closer to the scene, or had so many other details along with his description that it became clear he had a better memory. Or our reporter could simply report that the witnesses' descriptions varied widely. The latter sounds uncertain, but it is true. The reason the averaging in this example doesn't work is that there's a true answer to the robber's height, and five foot ten was almost assuredly not it. Saying so might have offered the comfort of not being too far *off* from his true height, whichever one it was. But to gain that comfort you have to deliberately trade away the likelihood of being precisely correct.

Each pollster does try to be as precise as he or she can. In this example "tall" and "short" are constructs we imposed on our description, just like "leading" and "trailing" are in a campaign. If all those reports suggested the robber was tall, say, over six feet, but varied in their specific assessments from six-two to six-nine, you'd have more confidence in at least saying he was "tall," if you so chose, if not specifically how tall.

When we use one of the polling aggregations we know we're treating each poll like a data point, and not all data points are equal, and not all are different because of randomness. There are differences in pollsters' points of view that aren't immediately clear how to reconcile. We've often preached that with data, more is better. That's true, but only when you collect all your data the same way.

Each poll is a study unto itself. The pollster decided whom to sample, how to ask the questions, who was likely to vote. The aggregators are well aware of this and many try to account for it by weighting the polls differently based on quality of methods and controlling for which ones might be real outliers, which appears to be helpful. (Nate Cohn of *The New York Times*, who helps run an aggregation himself, illustrated part of this dynamic once by giving the exact same raw interview data to different pollsters, who in turn sent back different vote estimates because each of them made reasonable, but different, choices in their design.)

Here's what I mean. Stop by a bar in Manhattan where, if my pollster friend Jim is in town, you might find us arguing about how to count a "likely voter" in our Ohio surveys. If you pull up a chair it would likely be one of the nerdiest conversations you're liable to hear in a bar. (I've made up Jim here as a stand-in for all the arguments pollsters really do have.) Jim runs a well-regarded poll, and for the sake of this example let's say he includes as a likely voter in Ohio anyone who says they're "probably" going to vote, and suppose he's got a good track record doing that. On the other hand, let's suppose in my poll I only include people who say they'll "definitely" vote, and I've got a good track record of my own. Jim's poll will probably have a different candidate choice number than mine, simply because he has a different group of people answering his question. His initial assumptions about the world—in this case, who'll vote in Ohio—are different from mine. Should you average us? I think instead you should decide which of us has offered you the better explanation of the world at the time and *pick* the one of us that does.

A good news organization will also do some of this for you. I'll certainly do my best. I try to think of it as part of good reporting—checking your sources, getting the best one, and showing the viewers that one, maybe at the exclusion of others, like the bank witness who just didn't have a good view. (Though if Jim's turns out to be closer, I guess I'm buying the next round.)

Sometimes the differences are a lot more extreme. This is where we pollsters sometimes cringe seeing our polls aggregated. I might not mind being averaged in with Jim's reliable poll. And the big networks, the newspapers, all of whom spend the resources and the time to get representative samples, that's fine company to keep. At times we'll also be averaged in with some firm that's never polled the race before, or maybe one that, just as an example, didn't dial cell phones—possibly missing more than half the population—or one with a strange imbalance of partisans or demographic groups that cannot be explained by a real-world influence. Those are mixed in the averages sometimes. They might be discounted in the aggregations, but they're in there nonetheless. If they are, I'll shy away from the average that results and I won't recommend reporting it out to you, because it mixes in kinds of polls that wouldn't otherwise meet our standards.

Chapter Twelve

Polling in the Present Tense

So what do you need to know?

There's yet another product out there for you, beyond polls, different from aggregations, and that's the *forecasts*, which communicate the idea of what *could* happen—and which are often taken as saying what *will* happen. These have long come from political scientists; there's one at *The New York Times*'s "Upshot" section, and in recent years perhaps most famously from Nate Silver's *FiveThirtyEight* website. They communicate ideas that handicap the election as in "the candidate has a 70 percent chance to win." The forecasts don't purport to be polls or surveys—the forecasters by and large don't interview anyone—though they include aggregations of other people's survey data in their product, along with other information like the state of the economy or demographics, to make forward-looking statements. They provide a very different service to the politics junkie.

A poll is not meant to be a forecast, and neither does a poll tell you who is *going* to win. Pollsters have tried to draw a distinction between themselves and forecasters for years but still get lumped together, for understandable reasons.

First, we do often both report our ideas as percentages, though there are very different ideas behind them.

Then, the leader in pre-election polls *does* end up winning often and so some people automatically—and erroneously—assume the leader in a poll will always win. Some pollsters have immodestly suggested polls became victims of their own success in that regard. It's more, I think, that we pollsters are all too happy to say when our last pre-election polls match an election result after the fact, but then we're quick to say "hey, it's not a prediction" when it's off, so it can just seem like we want it both ways.

Pollsters, being experts in people, claim to be able to pick out a voter from a nonvoter, but also know that people can be uncertain. Good forecasts do express uncertainty, but the public often misinterprets forecasts, too, as meaning a candidate is "going to win," especially when they put out a likelihood of an outcome up at something like 80 or 90 percent and higher.

But you will not likely—and should not, in my view—get poll reports from a reputable news pollster that uses the phrase "going to win" before Election Day when giving you their poll result. That's not our goal. I actually think the poll has more useful information than that.

It's What You Think—Not What You're Going to Think

A poll is different from a prediction because of what we're trying to tell you, and more importantly what we're not. The forecast tells you what could be. The poll tells you what is.

A poll does not put an outright probability on what you might or might not *think* in the future. I like to believe I know what you think now. But even you probably don't know what you're going to think down the road. I should know the range of options you would consider, if I've asked the right questions, and that can be essential. But I don't report a probability on your future choices among them. If I came on the *Evening News* and said there was an 80 percent chance people like you would switch from opposing the tax bill to supporting it next week, you'd rightly raise an eyebrow. If you're a conservative Republican and I said you'd become a liberal Democrat next month, boy, would my Twitter feed light up.

I'm a news pollster. I like to think people turn to us to explain what's happening, same as any news. A colleague who's a foreign correspondent wouldn't typically report her own analysis that the U.S. was "going to win" the war this year. She would say that U.S. troops were in a strong position and had seized key territory. Our transportation correspondent would certainly tell you if the FAA had declared an airport unsafe. They'd tell you if an accident had occurred. They wouldn't typically report that there probably *would be* an accident at the airport this week. That's not really what I believe people tune in to the *news* for.

Predictions and polls have gotten especially tied together with the rise of forecasting websites like Nate Silver's, but from my vantage point watching the races in 2008 and in 2012, it looked like Silver was using forecasting to make a larger point in favor of using data in and of itself—and by extension polling—as much for the sake of making a prediction.

In those years, the polls showed Barack Obama leading. Still, this idea challenged some of the received wisdom about politics. Some thought those polls had to be wrong because an African American candidate hadn't won the presidency before. In 2012, the narrative invited skepticism because the economy was still bad, and incumbents always lost when the economy was bad. That was history, just "how politics worked," or so some pundits thought.

Structural models of elections, which essentially say that macro conditions, like high unemployment, pointed against the polls, too, and hinted that a challenger would be favored. Pundits who paid attention to these ideas and basically ignored the current polling data, which said people were voting for Obama anyway, were falling back on what were essentially old models of the world. As news pollsters, we reported what we saw.

Silver, freed to make predictions, assembled it all into a single place, used that new information available—including the polls that pollsters were doing—modeled it into one number, and pushed back against that punditry, and those older ways of thinking, through the forecast. He presented it all as a sort of *preponderance of evidence* that the conventional wisdom was wrong, using the data and believing what people were saying in our polls, and thus updating prior information.

The real struggle comes when the forecast goes the other way, when something is unlikely and people misinterpret that as being impossible, but it happens anyway. A good forecast defines a range of all possibilities and their likelihood. But a close contest in the polling can apparently get magnified and show up as a gaping spread in a forecast, or at least that's what's happened lately. This invites a lot of confusion. *The New York Times*'s David Leonhardt, who headed the data-driven "Upshot" section at its inception, notes that probabilities are "inherently hard to grasp," that people simply want to know whether something will happen or not. Silver points out that most readers tend to make "errors of interpretation" on probabilities and underemphasize things with relatively smaller percentage chances of occurring, discounting them more than they already are. The very idea of expressing things in probabilistic terms is to express uncertainty, he explains, but too often everyone just wants to express things in quite the opposite fashion: as either yes or no.

Phil Tetlock and Dan Gardner in their book, *Superforecasting*, have a particularly fun explanation for why people tend to have only two settings in their quest for answers, yes or no, suggesting this tendency may naturally have descended to us from our ancestral thought processes. The caveman needed to know, they write, whether that shadow in the bush was a lion or not. "The ability to distinguish between a 60% probability" that it was a lion, and "an 80% probability would add little. In fact, a more fine-grained analysis could slow you down—and get you killed."

So this all has echoes, to me, in that overreliance on thinking of the poll horse race as win or lose.

Planning or Talking

I'm a bit biased in all this, of course, in whether one ought to pay more attention to forecasts or polls, and I'm all for the fine-grained explanation. Really, it once more depends on what you need to know: whether you need to plan for things, or you need to understand and affect things.

Tetlock and Gardner note "we are all forecasters" at times. "When we think about changing jobs, getting married, buying a home, making an investment, launching a product, or retiring, we decide based on how we expect the future will unfold." Being good at evaluating what will happen can have big payoffs. Everywhere throughout the world there are people whose job it is to plan, too. If you or your financial advisor reads a prospectus for stock you're thinking of buying, you'll surely want to know what the future trends are in sales or whatever they make. Sports teams, naturally, come to mind in this, too, as teams sign star free agents or find young prospects based on what they think they might do in the future, and an organization's whole future can hinge on the scouts that can pick out the future stars from the future duds. They all need to forecast.

How much we need to think like this for a presidential contest, though, can at best depend. Most have a rooting interest in it, most likely: for the sake of the country and maybe for long-term consequences that will affect you. Many might have been bitterly disappointed or utterly elated, but most people don't actively need to take steps *in advance* for the contingencies of that November vote. To be fair, some people might: they could be wagering actual, large sums of money on the contest. Some might only vote or volunteer if they fear their candidate is going to lose.

But people generally don't make those kinds of bets. And most probably did not make major decisions that hinged on knowing the election outcome, such as to start a business, or buy one industry's stock the summer before the vote, based on who they thought would win. Most people do not buy property someplace in October based on the way the campaign is going, though we always hear the hyperbole of people who claim they'll leave the country if the other side wins. (All of which is perhaps something of a testimony to the long-term stability of the American system.)

It's emotionally fun to feel like we know something, and guessing the future right can make us feel that we do. Tetlock and Gardner note that there's often a "comfort" aspect to forecasts, "assuring the audience that their beliefs are correct and the future will unfold as expected. Partisans are fond of these. . . . They are the cognitive equivalent of slipping into a warm bath."

I would humbly suggest you do not need that bath. Because you have agency. In politics, you're not just watching, rooting, or betting on an outcome from the stands, you're participating in something where the outcome isn't predetermined. Maybe that's in a small way with a vote, and maybe in a bigger way, out knocking on doors or running a town hall meeting, or trying to persuade others to see things your way, or just to vote themselves. You can change the outcome.

That's how it ought to be. I'm not sure we'd really want all the outcomes to be predicted. If everything could be predicted, then we'd all be predict-*able*. There'd be no need for those campaigns, no arguments, no persuasion—no one would ever come asking you for your view or your vote—because we'd all know what you thought before you even thought about it. That would be boring. Weird, even. Fortunately, it's not the case.

Consider that for all the election polls you see, most surveys go on behind the scenes helping people figure out which kinds of soap or cars or computers—and yes, in politics, which policies and candidates—you like. The company that made the computer I'm typing this on knows how many computers it sells, it knows the "score" in that sense. They also probably forecast how many more they'll sell if trends continue. But if they want to actually sell me one, and affect that trend, what they need to know is what affects me. They might ask me what I enjoy about a computer or why I want a nice screen—they'll learn my eyesight is already poor; too much time staring at numbers. So if there are a lot of people like me, that's a selling point they can emphasize in their ads to drive up sales. They learned something they can use through a survey.

A poll can be a dossier on democracy for you. It's actionable intelligence. Who might be persuaded? Who are they? How? Who's with and against you? How many are there, and where are they? Even if you just use that poll to understand the world better, see more of the pieces, then you're more informed in the big argument going on. You'll understand the landscape and all its parts. That's the information you need to know. What happens depends on what people like you actually decide to do.

So you might even use that poll to change someone's mind, now that you're seeing more of how they think. You may or may not, but you at least have, well . . . a chance.

Chapter Thirteen

The Politics of Inequality

At the beginning of the twenty-first century the CBS News poll asked people a simple question that embodies the American Dream: whether their own opportunities in life were better or worse than those of their parents.

The answers were overwhelmingly positive. Seventy-two percent said their chances were better, a paltry 5 percent said worse, and most importantly the optimism spanned age groups: it was as prevalent among the young as among anyone else. Three-quarters of those under thirty said their outlook was better.

But by 2007 the number of Americans who felt their chances were "worse" had tripled. Then the economy crashed and the recession raged, and by late 2009 that "worse" number was up, while the percentage who said their chances were "better" had nosedived. In 2014 the feeling that opportunities to succeed were worse had risen yet again, and in 2016 was still five times more negative than it had been in the year 2000.

In that 2016 poll, the same age cohort that we'd labeled as young back in 2000—between eighteen and twenty-nine years old—was now between their thirties and mid-forties. Now nearly a third of them said their chances in life were worse, a six-fold increase from what their cohort's answers had been at the start of the century. Under half of those aged thirty to forty-four said their opportunities were better, which was a plunge in optimism from the three quarters who'd said that back in 2000, when their cohort was still in their twenties. It looked like there was a generation of Americans entering their prime career and earning years with far less optimism than they'd held as they'd entered adulthood.

The idea of fairness in the economy, and government's perceived role in affecting it, was present at least from the beginning of the downturn. We saw empirically that disparities in income and wealth grew dramatically over recent decades, and particularly in recent years. The economic recovery was uneven at best.

The Bailout

A poll can gauge a lot of things fast: we want to know instant reactions to a speech; did voters love or hate the debate; what's the president's approval, right now, and again tomorrow. Over time, though, bigger things change; context changes, and major events reshape how we think, not just what we think. Sometimes it's worth taking a wider view and trying to understand how people process all that.

The 2008 crash did not look like a consequence of normal American boom-and-bust or cycles, whose inevitable peaks and valleys no one singlehandedly set, and which the nation tended to ride out together. So there were few clear comparisons in polling between the crash and the recessions of the early 1990s or 1980s.

Arguments began immediately over who got helped—and specifically, who deserved help—and who did not. The government was seen to be taking a side, and it wasn't the public's. Anger about who was helped spanned administrations. It started right away with skepticism about the government's response to the crisis, and then to the bailout, and displeasure only built over time.

In September of 2008, the CBS News poll found an initial and wide disconnect between who was being hurt by the crash—92 percent said the whole country was affected—and a majority who said only Wall Street would be helped by the bailout. Liberals, moderates, and conservatives were all split over whether the government ought to provide money to struggling financial institutions—in which only 13 percent had a lot of confidence—and by almost 20 points Americans believed it would be more of a burden on taxpayers than a way to stop the collapse of the economy.

A scant 2 percent had a lot of confidence that the money being used to bail out banks and financial institutions would actually help improve the economy. By the spring of 2009, views of the government's help to financial institutions had dropped again, and more said they felt "resentful" that "irresponsible" banks were getting money, more than felt relieved at the prospects that some of those institutions might start lending again, which was the intention of the policy. By a 30-point margin, Americans believed plans to help the nation's banking system would only benefit bankers; this was true of large majorities of conservatives and independents; and, despite the usual deference that a party's voters sometimes provide their president's policies, half of Democrats thought that as well. At least 80 percent of all partisans thought that the government should put a limit on the amount of money that senior executives at companies receiving bailout money could earn.

Blame for all the problems was harder to assign. There were bankers and bond raters and hedge fund managers who had once been celebrated—or at least unquestioned—as mavens of a modern economic system while they supplied seemingly unlimited money in the run-up to the crash, but who now were criticized for having been too lax or, perhaps, who had even nefariously caused the downturn. These ideas were complicated to poll on: few Americans could draw distinctions between various parts of the financial services industry, which is usually shortened as "Wall Street." Given the choice of which political party was more responsible, Americans overwhelmingly pointed to both.

Homeowners, meanwhile, were seen alternately as aspiring innocents who'd tried to buy a larger stake in society and who got caught up in a scheme, or irresponsible actors who had let their desire get ahead of their means. It was not clear among the millions of them who, exactly, was who.

As the mortgage crisis had started to unfold in the spring of 2008, we asked who was responsible, and the top answer was the "regulators," as Americans pointed to a government role right away, but as many blamed either borrowers or lenders. "Regulators" was the top answer among all partisan groups.

Americans themselves, though, reported being directly and negatively affected right away. In February of 2009 the number of people calling the economy bad hit a record high in the poll at 94 percent, and a third of the nation said the crash had already forced them to change personal long-term plans; four in ten Americans reported being negatively affected by the falling real estate market, and a quarter knew someone who'd filed for bankruptcy or had a foreclosure.

By February 2009 the bailout was still viewed negatively by Americans, even more so than it had been at the end of 2008.

The stimulus package did not fare especially well either. It got mixed reviews largely along partisan lines, but only one in five Americans believed it would shorten a recession that most expected to linger for years.

In early summer 2009, only 19 percent thought the package was helping their community. By 2010, over a third felt the whole U.S. economy was in permanent decline.

CBS polled about who was to blame for the crash, offering Americans an "open-ended" question where they could answer anything or anyone they liked rather than choose from a list we gave, and the answers were always a mixed bag between political figures and Wall Street. In 2009, when we offered the question with a discrete list of choices, the combined set of political figures—including Congress, and former President Bush—came in slightly higher than the choice of "Wall Street and financial companies" among all Americans, though when we looked at it by partisan breakdowns, Wall Street was among the top answers for partisans of all stripes.

Uneven

Then the recovery, as it slowly took hold, was uneven, with the already better-off getting a disproportionate share of the gains in the rebound by multiple measures. Inequality was rising.

Americans noticed. In 2011 nearly seven in ten said they thought the rich were getting richer. In 2015 two-thirds of them said money and wealth ought to be more evenly distributed in the country. Only 30 percent said it was fair as it was. As of 2017 the top 1 percent owned nearly 39 percent of the nation's wealth. The Pew Research Center showed that in 2017 "wealth gaps between upper-income families and lower- and middle-income families are at the highest levels recorded." Most of the new jobs came in places that were already more prosperous. Even as unemployment went lower by traditional measures, many of the new jobs created were not paying as well, were temporary, and didn't have benefits.

In fact, the recession and slow recovery had only exacerbated a long-term trend. The middle- and lower-class families had not participated in economic growth in the last three decades as they had a generation before. From 1991 to 2010 the proportion of U.S. adults in the middle income of households shrank, while that proportion had expanded in some other Western nations.

It started to feel like some of those older measures of "how" the economy was doing were incomplete in this context. Polls had to take into account ways in which Americans absorbed this new reality. People might have decided it was all just a transient change in their economic status, or else, perhaps, a change in how the economy fundamentally operated, and a symptom of a larger trouble; not how things were *doing*, but how things *worked*. Or even whether the system could work in the first place.

It looked like the latter. In the summer of 2010, the poll asked very simply who could get ahead in the U.S. economy and almost two-thirds said only those at the top, a view that would still be the same in the summer of 2016. In the general election of 2012, a 55 percent majority of voters had said the U.S. economy favored the wealthy and fewer thought it was "fair to all Americans." In our polling, by 2015 people under forty-five were unlikely to believe that the economy was fair to everyone, with most of them saying that it was not, and a majority of older Americans didn't see an economy that worked, either. For them, having spent prime years though the expansions of the 1980s and 1990s, it may have looked more like an economy that had once worked and had since slipped away. Put as a slightly different question to Americans in the winter and spring of 2017, Was the U.S. economy fair or not fair?, a similar 59 percent said the U.S. economy was unfair.

Americans' longer-term outlook for the next generation grew cloudier as well. In the recession, the percentage of parents who thought their children's standard of living would someday be worse than their own had risen.

Middle Class Voting

The 2012 Republican presidential primaries were the first national intraparty contests to take place after the crash, and if the narrative was focused on the inevitable winner, Mitt Romney, or whether he was conservative enough, it would have missed the stirrings of a split along economic lines that would echo into 2016. Romney struggled among lower-income Republicans even as he became the prohibitive favorite for the nomination. Ron Paul had initially handily won voters earning under $50,000 in the Iowa caucuses that opened the nominating season, and in the later part of the primaries, Rick Santorum stayed in contesting states into the spring and it was he, not Romney, who won lower-income voters in Michigan and Ohio, even as Romney ran up large leads with Republicans earning over $100,000. At the Decision Desk that year, as the primaries wore on, we were able to build predictive models of the Romney primary vote by county by relying heavily not just on past votes, nor even on ideology, but on housing value data from the Census by county. Romney did best where wealth was higher and worse where it wasn't.

Then in the 2012 general election, one-third of Republican voters—even as they backed Romney against Obama—echoed that idea that the U.S. economy favored the wealthy. Two years later, in the 2014 midterms, even as the Republican Party sailed to gains in the Senate and House, we noted that the percentage saying the economy favored the wealthy jumped to 42 percent of Republican voters. This was especially notable because midterm elections feature the most reliable partisans. The feeling of unfairness had grown. The Democrats did not have contested primaries in 2012 as President Obama ran for reelection, but Democratic rank-and-file dissatisfaction was still apparent four years into their hold on the White House: 79 percent of those who backed Obama that year said that the economy unfairly favored the wealthy.

With all the data showing how the recovery was affecting people so differently by income, it made sense to keep an eye on how people of different means were responding.

In our recent polls, only among people who consider themselves upper- or upper-middle-class does a majority believe the economy works fairly, and even then it is just a slim majority. Those in the middle and lower classes largely considered the economy to be unfair. It defines a large group of Americans not only working day to day to make ends meet but, by this measure anyway, believing they are doing all that within the confines of a system stacked against them.

Americans often have different conceptions of which voters the parties represent than the ones they actually do, at least in terms of coalitions if not policy. Most Americans have long considered themselves middle-class, almost regardless of their income, and so most political rhetoric talks about ways to help the middle class. Yet very few Americans see either party as aligned exclusively with the middle. A small 12 percent in 2017 felt the Republicans favor the middle class over other groups and a mere 19 percent think the Democrats do; fewer than half of Americans think either one of them favored the middle class or at least treated all groups the same.

A majority of Americans saw the Republican Party in particular as representing the rich, with only a quarter thinking Republicans at least treat all groups—rich, middle class, and poor—equally. The perception that the GOP favors the rich is especially pronounced among their opponents, with more than eight in ten Democrats thinking so, and most independents agreeing. That doesn't always preclude people from voting for them, of course, partly because the Democrats are hardly immune from this perception, too. A quarter of Americans think the Democrats favor the wealthy, and many Republicans were likely to describe the Democratic Party that way. In fact, it's the most prevalent answer Republicans give when describing the Democratic Party, even more so than saying they believe Democrats favor the poor. This reflects part of the perception among their detractors that the Democratic Party is increasingly associated with an urban elite concentrated along the coasts.

The reality of who actually forms each party's coalition, though, is much more spread out. The percentage of each party's coalition is actually composed similarly between income groups. The Democrats' coalition and the Republicans' coalition are each composed of about one-third from voters in $100,000 households; among the Democrats' voters, 39 percent earned under $50,000, and among Republican voters 32 percent did.

In their congressional delegations, both parties are heavily reliant on relatively lower- and working-class voters. If we control for race and look at white voters who have fallen in the lower bracket of the poll's income breaks in any given year, earning under $50,000 at the time of the election, they look like the swing group that they are. Big Republican gain years like 1994 and 2010 have come when they've done relatively well with lower-income white voters, and Democrats, in turn, have done well nationally when they've done well with these same voters. As Democratic voters clustered around expensive cities and the coasts, congressional Democrats represented more of the wealthiest and higher-income districts, as well as some with wide disparities in income that one finds in and around cities like New York, Boston, or San Francisco. Republican-held congressional districts as of 2017 had relatively lower median income and median home value compared to Democratic-held ones, as the Republican congressional coalition is more rural as well as suburban.

Splits Inside the Parties

Inside each party we've seen a sizable number of discontented partisans on these measures. In the spring of 2016 Bernie Sanders led Hillary Clinton among Democratic primary voters on who could better handle inequality. In the 2016 New Hampshire primary, as Bernie Sanders won handily, he beat Clinton by nearly 30 points among the Democratic primary voters who said the U.S. economy favored the wealthy. Sanders would consistently beat Clinton among whites who said the economy wasn't fair in state after state. Even as their party held the White House, Democratic primary voters consistently said the U.S. economy favored the wealthy.

Among Democrats, the view that the economy is unfair is much more widespread and less correlated with education and income. Upper- and lower-income Democrats today are equally likely to think Wall Street hurts the economy more than it helps. This view is more connected to ideology. The relatively fewer Democrats who see a fair economy call themselves more moderate and those who see unfairness call themselves liberal.

Among Republicans, even once their party controlled the White House, Senate, and House of Representatives in 2017, one-third still said the economy was unfair, and they were lower in socioeconomic status: nearly half with only high school educations, a higher percentage than Republicans overall; and they tended toward the lower end of the income scale. They were comparably less likely to believe the American Dream is still attainable. Many of their economic policy views run counter to more traditional Republican ideology. A majority said government should do *more* to solve problems. Six in ten said Wall Street's practices hurt the economy. Seventy percent of them said government favored the rich. (They did share cultural ideas with other Republicans, though. They're just as apt to dislike "political correctness." Most of all they did not like liberals, and gave them exceedingly low rankings on a list of groups to like or dislike.)

Expensive and Exclusive

I was sitting in on a focus group in St. Louis that we were doing for *Face the Nation*, on the eve of one of the 2016 presidential debates. The group was a mix of hardened liberals and conservatives, gathered in the main room of a stately law library that was lit in a honey-hued glow for the cameras. Two older men, one conservative, the other liberal, had been firmly trading arguments on everything and anything and doing their best, successfully, to show restraint in front of an audience, but I wondered if things might have gotten a lot louder had they been in a less reserved setting—though it was more likely that they would never have had a conversation at all. Then the topic *Citizens United* came up— the court case that many voters blame for letting too much money into politics. Both men announced they hated it, so much so they reflexively stood up and shook hands, seeming as happy to have made a friend as to let out the tension between them. "Now *that* we can agree on!" they smiled. And that, I thought, is the first time I've seen people bond by shouting out the name of a court case, and one about campaign expenditures, no less.

The connective thread between government and economic unfairness kept appearing to be big-money donors, the political class, gaming the system, pushing policies that made things unfair. I knew that in the states we tested in 2016, Donald Trump led Hillary Clinton by a wide margin on which candidate would listen to regular people as opposed to listening to big donors. And I knew that the donors issue was one of the biggest defining splits among primary choices for Republicans in 2016 in the first place: on the eve of Super Tuesday, for instance, the largest collection of state primary and caucus votes of the year, seven in ten Republicans felt Trump would side with regular people over them. I also knew that Bernie Sanders had held dramatic leads over Clinton on who would listen to average people versus donors. Big donors have never been popular in politics, of course, but it seemed liked the unequal outcomes of the economy looked more and more to people like the tangible results of their influence on government. It was all still a little nebulous, though, and maybe a little convenient; an idea that could explain everything from trade policy to immigration policy, if people wanted it to.

I like to get as many views and stories in as I can to try to piece all this together. I was sharing some of my focus group stories with David Winston from our Decision team, who runs a lot of his own polls around the country. Winston came up as a policy wonk more than a pollster, working on tax and economic policy at the Heritage Foundation in the 1990s. He got involved with Election Nights through Murray Edelman back in 1998, calling congressional races, but his focus remains economic issues. I look to him for reads on pragmatic, pocketbook voters, a counterpoint to the view that everyone out there is voting to change the world.

He describes listening recently to a well-meaning, middle-aged gentleman in a midwestern town who'd been forced to shift from job to job and lamenting that he would never have a single good one that he could retire from. It was more than just about a paycheck, though that was paramount. This was a man thinking about the whole arc of his life. "He recognized the challenges he faced," David recounts, as his skill set had become obsoleted and he was desperately trying to stay in the workforce through sheer will." *Obsoleted.* That word caught me. The man David described wasn't seeing himself as a victim, per se, but felt that the economy and politics and the way they both worked had made things much more difficult for him. There was a more powerful group that was devaluing his role in society. "They take the governing away from the average person and they override our vote," as David recalled another group saying. "They" were elites. They'd been defined not by some partisan label, but rather by their resources. "They" were the people with time and money to be involved in politics, to influence the system in their favor. These ordinary, non-elite folks felt overridden.

Months later in a bar on a frigid night in New Hampshire, I listened to another group of voters hit this theme again as they batted around descriptions of connections between big money and government, and how—and this was taken as fact—some had more political access and resources to affect outcomes than they did.

Conversations all had this theme around who had say, or who had voice, and who didn't. In a 2017 survey, I gave people a list of ways to describe how they felt about their place in America generally, words like "empowered" or "influential" or "voiceless" or "forgotten." I figured I'd get some partisan-tinged responses, as these were very expansive words, but I tried it anyhow. Eighty-three percent of people who said that they felt "voiceless" in society also said the U.S. economic system favored the wealthy. Even among self-identified Republicans, whose party was in power, the people who thought the U.S. economic system favors the wealthy were the most likely of all Republicans to say they felt more generally "forgotten" and "voiceless" and only one in ten said they felt influential or empowered. The same patterns were true among independents and among Democrats—those feeling the system favored the wealthy were more apt to feel voiceless than those who said it was fair.

This idea of voice was interesting to me because we know that's one reason people vote, and take the time to get involved in the first place.

For the people we met, it was not that they necessarily begrudged others' money or that they resented expensive things, per se; everyone knows some things are pricey. But by definition, expensive also means exclusive, and in political life, specifically—in public life—they did not like feeling excluded. Whether this frustration leads to particular suspicion of large corporations, or of government, or those who they believed shipped jobs away, or enticed foreign labor, or got tax breaks, people's basic idea that they didn't have enough say has cut across a lot of the usual political divides.

Because people look for explanations about the world they see around them. And because they always want a voice.

Chapter Fourteen

Would You Invite a Democrat to Dinner?

When I was growing up everybody argued about politics, and the dinner table was the main debate stage. (There was no argument about grandma's cooking, of course.) Politicians' names were tossed about and gossiped over like any other set of familiar friends or family who weren't there to defend themselves. Or maybe *because* they weren't there to defend themselves. We usually had a mix of Democrats and Republicans and some that I'd now recognize as swing voters around the table depending on who'd dropped by that day, though my recollection is that none of those labels seemed to mean as much as they do today.

Family legend has it my dad and grandfather even liked to raise the stakes on occasion with side bets over various political outcomes, usually dinners out at the restaurant of the winner's choice where all this would just continue in a new venue. The most extravagant came back in 1974, over whether Richard Nixon would be impeached, with my staunchly Republican grandfather dutifully taking the "no" side as part of the scant 24 percent of Americans still supporting him that summer—and which in turn was surely what goaded my dad into pushing for that wager. Technically, Grandpa won when Nixon resigned and was pardoned instead. He paid up anyway. Grandpa was a stand-up guy.

Old surveys used to ask respondents how they'd feel about the idea of someone coming to dinner as a way of measuring social acceptance, or tolerance: how would you feel if someone in your family brought a person *different* from you home for dinner? It was used to get at racial views back in the 1960s and 1970s—views that respondents might not otherwise have expressed out loud. In a more lighthearted vein, political polls ask which candidate you'd invite over for dinner, or even just have a beer with, as a proxy for figuring out which one people just personally liked or didn't.

I was curious what would happen if we asked something like this of partisans today. Suppose, we posited, they were hosting a dinner where they knew politics was sure to come up in the conversation. Who would they like to have over: a mix of Democrats and Republicans, or just people in the same party as they themselves?

We got a mix. Half of partisans, Republicans and Democrats, wanted to invite people of the other party, and half did not. When we looked more closely, it was the strongest ideologues, in each party, who were the ones that didn't want different-thinking people around the table. The further left or right you went on the ideological scale, the more conservative or liberal people got, the more they only wanted to have people like themselves.

Of the Democrats who called themselves liberal, and in particular very liberal, 62 percent said they'd invite only people with the same politics.

Of Republicans who called themselves conservative, and in particular those who called themselves very conservative, 66 percent would invite only people with the same politics.

Now I do recognize not everybody wants a dinner party where the guests might argue—many might simply find that impolite, and understandably so. Not everyone thinks arguments are as interesting as my family did, and I'm certainly not claiming we were normal. On the other hand, maybe we could take this as a sign that these ideologues just don't like, or want to hear from, the others who disagree, and in either case it didn't seem to bode too well for democracy. Maybe it was better for indigestion. In 2017 Americans told us, by two to one, that conversations about politics were getting harder to have.

When another of our polls asked Americans about the overall tone and civility in politics nowadays, two-thirds felt that it had gotten worse in recent years.

How Different?

Surely anyone who has followed politics in recent years could be forgiven for thinking so. It's often assumed that our political choices now mark deeper cultural differences, maybe intractable ones. We have those now ubiquitous labels of "Red America" for conservative areas—and people—and "Blue America," for liberals, which both denote and connote supposed divisions and ways of life that go deeper than just what policies we want.

Campaigns, for their part, have always had something nasty to say about their political opponents, but nowadays even their supporters can get dragged in, too, usually in unflattering terms. New Yorkers heard Senator Ted Cruz in the 2016 primaries trying to appeal to conservatives in the Midwest by decrying people with "New York values." (Cruz lost New York, in case you wondered.) San Franciscans and Northeasterners, where liberal politics hold sway, often get similar geographic callouts from the right. It was Hillary Clinton referring to Donald Trump's supporters as "deplorables," and then many Trump backers in turn wearing that label like a badge of honor, relishing the distinction of being apart from the other groups backing her. The implicit choice in an election becomes framed not just between competing parties and candidates and ideas, but between peoples; not so much about what you want, as about who you are, or at least which of the groups alongside you in society you want to put into power or keep out of it. Then, when politics turns to the day-to-day dealings of governing, how are people supposed to find common ground with people whose entire way of life is—supposedly—so completely and utterly different from yours?

So let me ask you to try something: when you get to the end of this paragraph, close your eyes for a moment. If you're conservative, I'd like you to try picturing a liberal voter, whatever image of such a person springs to mind. What do they look like, and where are they? If you're liberal, imagine someone you'd think of as a typical conservative voter. And if you're more of a moderate, take an extra second, and try imagining both people on the left and right.

Okay, open up. What popped into your head? Conservatives: was the liberal you pictured in the city, dressed like a hippie, or maybe a hipster, smugly stepping out of a Prius and into a coffeehouse for a six-dollar latte? (The beans roasted by solar power, of course.) Liberals: did the conservative look like a retiree in a Sun Belt subdivision, sporting an angry scowl and a trucker hat while climbing into their pickup?

Or maybe you didn't think of caricatures like this at all. Maybe the images I just described sound like they're in some movie that you didn't see. That's fine. Did you think instead of someone you knew *personally*: your uncle whose ramblings about the state of the country leave you bemusedly entertained, at least for a little while; or the best friend you love like a sister, but who still makes everyone uncomfortably quiet whenever she brings up politics? That's fine, too, and maybe telling. There could be an important difference in whether you came up with an image that felt more like a "what," as opposed to a "who."

Red and Blue Places

Like a lot of people following politics, I've been interested in this idea of a divided America for a while, not so much because of crazy family dinners but, from a pollster's perspective, because it's a challenging concept to measure. What exactly defines divided?

Unlike the opinions that come directly from you, the cultural divide feels more high-concept, often described by our looking at broader voting trends, and measured in the aggregate as much as the personal.

Some see it in big colored charts and maps in newsrooms, the stark separation of northeastern and western coastal states won by Democrats and lit in "blue," and the whole of the South and mountain states in a solid Republican "red." The etymology traces to Election Night television and how we color the states for party winners. The use of the terms "polarization" and then "red state" and "blue state" spiked after 2000 and in the run-up to the 2004 contest. But like any labels, they stuck because they seemed to tell a larger and more intuitive story, this one supposedly about the people in those places. Some said geography did in fact explain it. Bill Bishop showed in his book *The Big Sort* that Americans had been increasingly living in—and moving into—counties that voted in lopsided fashion for either Republicans or Democrats. The total number of Americans living in these "landslide counties" was growing, suggesting that more and more of us were living near people who voted and thought the same way as we did. As the decade-long housing boom in the mid-'00s was taking Americans out into sprawling, far-flung new housing developments, a 2006 book titled *Applebee's America* described the "exit ramp" communities and spread-out towns that may not have been as physically conducive to community. Where people live can impact how we think of them, too, as political scientist Ryan Enos puts it in *The Space Between Us*, that "people use space as a mental shortcut . . . to help them organize the world and decide what they think of other groups."

Personal connections—especially connections between different kinds of people—matter. They make for a functioning democracy in the first place, one where people get along and govern themselves despite disagreements. Democracy, as scholars suggest, doesn't just depend on words on a paper constitution or a set of rules imposed from above. It comes from regular people gaining trust in others and social skills from day-to-day dealings, anyplace they need to negotiate or cooperate with people, in all aspects of their lives, including ones that aren't expressly political, like in business, trade, social groups, and community organizations. As people become practiced and trusting in these ways and means and interactions, they come to accept a larger political life that's more dynamic and open to discussion.

The Other People

What was happening in terms of territory has been happening in the minds of partisans, too. The parties are now filled with more ideologues than they used to be.

The CBS News poll has been asking people whether they're conservative, moderate, or liberal for forty years. In the 1980s Republicans were split between conservatives and moderates. Since then the conservative composition of Republicans has risen to around 70 percent today.

Among Democrats, liberals have been on the increase, a slow but steady upswing over the decades. The Democrats had, on average, slightly more moderates than liberals in the party until around the late 2000s and it fluctuated around 2014, but the overall trend line from the decades now shows liberals slightly more. Parties, in the classic sense, have long been thought of as coalitions of disparate interest groups stitched together by a thing or two in common. But on this self-identity measure at least, they appear increasingly as collections of like-minded people, or at least people who share a common view for themselves.

Then there are the views of the parties themselves. We already know partisans don't cross over and vote for each other much anymore, but there's also just growing disdain and dislike when they think about the label. They've never actually *liked* each other of course, so all this is relative, but it's become nearly absolute. In the 1990s, and until the early 2000s—around that time of the red-blue attention—Republicans averaged a 72 percent unfavorable view of the Democratic Party, and now that's up to 88 percent. In the 1990s, Democrats had an unfavorable view of the Republicans around the low-70-percent range as well, and now they've consistently shown negative views in the high-80-percent range over the last few years.

All these measures felt like top-down analyses, though. I had wondered how to get more personal and see if it was something in the eye of the beholder and not the beholden, to what extent this idea of a divide was something that regular people saw in themselves, or just something we were seeing in our fancy maps and trend lines. Pollsters like to trace ideas back to people. In other words, how would we even know a "divided" person if we surveyed one?

Staring Across the Divide

The 2004 election was my presidential first at CBS and I felt like I'd dropped right into this emerging culture divide debate. After it, I asked respondents on one of our national polls an open-ended question, one that doesn't give a set list of answer choices but lets the respondent say whatever they want in their own words. We asked people to tell us in their own words what the labels "conservative" and "liberal" meant to them.

What struck me was getting so few policy-related answers, and so many more personal ones. We didn't get mentions of the federal budget, or details about Social Security, or abortion, or even marriage. Mostly what I got described large-scale differences in people's perceived approach to the wider world and their decision making in general. It was certainly in keeping with the idea of these labels being as much about identity as about policy. "Conservatives are cautious and liberal means you don't hold anything back," said one; "Conservatives are more traditional, old-fashioned, and liberals more contemporary," went another.

Overall, Americans' descriptions of "liberals" in the abstract depicted a group that was thought of as emotional (either for better or worse) or tolerant (again, for better or worse, if the latter meant they were overly permissive) and, often, open-minded or accepting of change; more disparagingly, but in the same vein: reactionary or rash. "Conservatives," in turn, were called thoughtful (as opposed to reactionary) in positive comments, though to some that had a negative connotation of being too slow; traditional (again, for better or worse), empowering the individual and religiously oriented; or in more disparaging judgments about the same general notion, liberals called conservatives intolerant, closed-minded, and too stuck in their ways.

Americans' descriptions of each other also gave us more fun and snark than we could find in just data. "Liberals will give you the shirt off their back," quipped one conservative poll respondent, "and then charge you for it." A liberal respondent painted conservatives as people who could afford the luxury of caring about abstract ideas. "Conservative views are for people who don't have to worry about making payments on their furniture."

Who Are Those People?

After the 2016 contest—where rancor had only seemed to have gotten worse—and then throughout 2017, I started asking division questions to our CBS News Nation Tracker panel. On "feeling thermometers" where respondents are asked to scale their affinity for groups from "like a lot" to "dislike intensely," the very conservative and the very liberal tended to give the other side the lowest feeling scores they were allowed to give.

It was clear conservatives and liberals had different ways of seeing the world, not only each other. Given the choice, conservatives were likely to say they saw the world as "clearly divided into forces that are good and forces that are evil," while liberals tended to pick the description that said "the world is complicated, and ideas of good and evil depend on where you stand."

The very conservative and the very liberal are also more likely to describe themselves as surrounded by like-minded people, by friends and family of the same political views. The differences between them and those who call themselves just "somewhat" liberal and "somewhat" conservative are dramatic. Forty percent of the very liberal, and 41 percent of the very conservative, said most friends and family around them shared their views, but only 27 and 24 percent, respectively, of the "somewhat" liberal and conservative said so. Intensity of ideology was related to being around more people like yourself.

But then we asked people to look across the divide and describe the people who disagreed with them, not merely by whether or not you liked them, but what kind of people you thought they were, beyond politics. We asked conservatives about liberals, and liberals about conservatives, and asked them to tell us specifically if they believed the other side at least *shared basic values and life goals with them apart from politics*. I felt like I set this bar pretty low. Or, did they believe people who held political differences also meant those opponents did not share "other values or goals"? I figured this was one way to just let people define the so-called cultural divide for themselves, just ask people if they saw differences in each other that were defined by—but went beyond—just politics.

Within each group of ideologues, about six in ten of those who call themselves liberals and two-thirds of conservatives, felt their political opponents were very different people from them in other ways *besides* politics, too. But the remainder of each said the differences stopped with politics—that people of the opposing ideology probably *did* share other values and goals in life with them.

So despite widespread dislike between most ideologues, others sensed or assumed some basic commonality in life across the political divide.

So let's take the ones who say they don't see commonality, and put them into perspective, what part of the whole country they are, by this basic measure. In these terms, it's just over one-third of the country who do two important things in term of "division": they think of themselves in ideological terms, liberal or conservative, and then *also* think of people of the opposing ideology as entirely different kinds of people, with differences extending beyond politics. Let's call them the *divide-minded*. They see a division in the country that goes beyond politics.

There are fewer who are ideologues themselves but believe their differences with the other side are confined to politics; that there is commonality besides politics. This is 11 percent of the country who are liberal and think they do have some connections with conservatives, and 11 percent who are conservatives returning the favor to liberals, for a total of 22 percent of the whole. Let's call them the *connection-minded* ideologues. They disagree and mostly dislike the other side, but assume there is something shared with their opponents beyond those political lines.

That's what cultural division looks like to people, in basic form.

> Divide-minded ideologues (conservative or liberal) who think
>> the other side does *not* share things in common beyond politics:
> 37 percent.
> Connection-minded ideologues (conservative or liberal) who *do*
>> see commonality aside from politics: 22 percent.
> Everyone else (nonideologues, moderates, unsure): 41 percent.

The divide-minded ideologues are also a bit more likely to describe a more homogenous group of like-minded political thinkers around themselves. Familiarity on a personal level may breed a sense of connection, or at least goes hand in hand with it: if you hang around with people who think differently than you do, you're more likely to see them as having shared values outside of politics. If they aren't around, they're different. They're abstractions. We see this same pattern among both conservatives and liberals.

We don't really know whether this is a cause or an effect. It could be they've chosen over time to only surround themselves with people of similar political views, intentionally pushing aside others, or it could be that their surroundings cause their views: the fact that they were surrounded by only one kind of people and that has led to their suspicion of others. That's a long personal history to disentangle, so we just kept it simple and asked if they wanted to live around people of different kinds of political persuasions, or around people of the same, if they had the choice. On this, there were differences among conservatives. Two-thirds of the conservative *divide-minded* respondents said they preferred to live mainly around people like just themselves. This view was not as large for those who did see commonality with liberals, who were more inclined to want different political groups around them.

We asked a very broad question about how the world works, with no mention of politics or label for "people" in it: whether you believe that most other people try to be fair in their dealings with you and others, or whether most people in the world would take advantage of you if they could. The divide-minded ideologues were generally less trusting of others in general, more likely to feel that other people would take advantage of them if those others could, as opposed to the idea that most other people generally try to act fairly. This dynamic was true for the "divided" among both liberals and conservatives.

The demographics among the divided and connected aren't dramatically different. The connection-minded tend to be a little younger, the divide-minded a little older, but nothing really jumps out when comparing them on gender, race, or education; they're much the same. This looked like more of a state of mind. There is an ideological divide, but there is also a split between those who perceive division in the first place, and those who don't.

More, or More Involved?

The divide-minded ideologues, as I've defined them here, make up far less than half the population, and viewed from that angle, it might seem surprising that people who think or appear to act on this idea could dominate politics at all if they are not in the majority.

So we asked why they get involved in politics in the first place, why they associated with a political party (the conservatives overwhelmingly with the Republicans and liberals with the Democrats). We know that the parties were getting increasingly filled up by ideologues. The divide-minded ideologues were comparatively a bit more focused on personal and group-based, or affinity-based, reasons to be in a party. They were more likely than those who saw connections to say they associate with parties to support people like themselves and more likely to say they joined specifically "to oppose the other side." So the very reason for feeling attachment to a party, in more group terms and opposition terms, rises along with seeing the other side as different people. This might dovetail with what political scientists call negative partisanship, the idea that it isn't so much they like their own party, but dislike the other.

Voter turnout and political participation is connected to caring, and to one's feeling that you can and must change things around you. The reported rate of participation in the presidential elections of 2012 and 2016 is slightly higher for the divide-minded. A majority of both types vote, but those who don't see connections were five points more likely to do so.

People who don't see connections across the divide are not the majority. They may just be the more active voices.

We asked everyone: "Do you feel American culture and society respect people like you, for who you are?" It was an intentionally broad idea. Most of the people who thought their opponents did in fact share common values also believed that they, themselves, were respected in society.

And most of the people who thought the other side didn't share their values—believed they, themselves, were not respected.

Maybe that's a big part of the explanation, too. Division is defined by how we see each other. And maybe knowing that is a way in—an invitation to talk.

All the People You Don't Know

It's never been easier to believe that we already know something—or, just as importantly, someone. Today everyone can pick and choose the news they want to hear; take in the stories that fit with their worldview, follow the agreeable sources and ignore the rest. In all these places we get portrayals—some implicit and some explicit, some correct and many distorted—of all those other Americans, all those other people out there; the ones we don't know.

That's a challenge for pollsters, maybe even more than getting some number right. It's a test for anyone who sets out to really show us who we are. We're pushing up against a lot of preconceptions. Maybe the challenge isn't so much convincing people they can know the world from just one of our little samples. Maybe it's that people think they've already seen it all.

But it's still worth pushing. To that end, here I've shown you some of how we do polls in the first place and how, like any science, the way that we do them changes, and that what we learn along the way changes, too. What I really hope I've shown you, though, is that for all the technical talk we hear around "the polls" of interviews and phones and the Internet and vote models, those are merely mechanisms, the parts of a tool; the microscope for the chemist; the telescope for the astronomer. They're really important, but like the very poll itself, they're just a means to an end. They aren't what we want to *know*.

What we want to *know* is what's going on; we want to understand what's out there, right now, in a world that's driven by what people think and do.

Finding that out isn't just about what tool you reach for, it's about an approach and a way of thinking. It's figuring out how you'll piece together whatever it is you begin to see. It's thinking about *how* people might think; finding the patterns in the numbers we get, and in what people say. And it's also about respecting the limits of what we can do; that sometimes we have to be satisfied with being in the ballpark, or with things being a little ambiguous or uncertain, and that it's still pretty remarkable we can get close in the first place.

Mostly, I hope you've seen that in a good poll, the story should be greater than the sum of the parts. Demand that from your pollster, if you didn't already. Every poll finding should pass the Rule of Because. "Americans favor the policy *because* . . ." "Opponents of the bill don't like it *because* . . ." For every number, your pollster should be ready with an explanation, not just of how it was calculated but of why it happens in the public mind. And the right number is usually the one that makes sense on both those fronts.

There's a good reason we want to know what's going on. Because while it's obvious that different people out there see things differently than we do, deep down we suspect that's probably not because they "don't know stuff" or they're "just partisan" or they're all good or all bad, no matter what the politics says or how convenient it can feel to sum it up that way. We know they have different considerations, a context; a shortcut; maybe ones you haven't thought of yet, or don't use yourself. They're familiar with some things and unfamiliar with others. It's just a little harder sometimes to see what, exactly. But if we ask, the right way, they'll probably tell us all about it. A good poll *should* ask them.

When a poll does that, it helps us follow a campaign like a campaign, not as a scoreboard tally; not something you're watching, but as a persuasion contest—one that you have a say in. One that you can affect. Maybe just by talking to somebody. Sometimes it's as simple as that. That's how a good poll starts.

The polls do show us stories of mistrust, and of intractability. There's no question there's plenty of that out there among the public. But stories of shared ideas and of change are there, too, along with some stories that are a little of both, where we aren't sure which way they'll go. It all looks like empirical evidence that where there are people, there are all sorts of possible outcomes.

But we've also seen that when people are predictable, we get predictable outcomes—and politics will take advantage of that.

Pollsters have long argued that our value is to tell the powerful what the people think, that poll numbers keep leadership—whoever it is—responsive, if not responsible. Maybe.

Today it might be more necessary for something that tells us what's true about ourselves, that paints a picture of those who agree and disagree in a way that offers a little more explanation and a little less suspicion. A democracy may or may not always respond to what we think, but it surely depends on what we think of each other.

So there's also great opportunity here. There's never been more information out there about everyone. There'll be demand for people who can make some sense of it. Polls are actionable intelligence; when you know why people think as they do, you can have a better conversation, or a better understanding, or a better shot at persuasion, if you feel like giving that a try.

Someone is going to use it. Someone is going to try to figure you out, put together what they think they know about you. Maybe to sell you something. Maybe to divide you from others. Or, perhaps, to foster a discussion.

Let's end on the last of those. When I've asked Americans if leaders should work for just their own voters, or for everyone, even the people whose party holds power have said: everyone. Americans overwhelmingly say they want more unity. Maybe those are just the right things to say. Maybe that idea means too many different things to different people to be practical; unity on some terms and not others. But it feels like a start.

Last year, 55 percent of Americans said they were optimistic the country could come together.

Fifty-five percent is not everyone.

But 55 percent is *most*.

So what will you make of that number?

Getting the Midterms "Right"—And on to 2020

By November of 2018, as the midterm elections neared and we were get-
ting ready for another long night at the Decision Desk, the pre-election
polls had already created expectations for what might happen in the
Senate and the House races. The Republicans were going into Election
Night with an edge to hold on to their Senate majority, and maybe add
to it, while on the House side, the Democrats were positioned to gain
seats and—provided turnout was high, we thought—take over control.
It would indeed turn out that way.

But the story that set up those expectations—and what we'd learned
from polling since I'd last walked off, bleary-eyed, from the Decision
Desk two years earlier—was once again more telling than just who won
and lost.

Back when President Trump had taken office in January 2017, there were repeated references from pundits and pollsters to the president's "base," ostensibly those Americans solidly approving of him, and also to those who were immediately and seemingly firmly opposed. Though we saw right away that was marked by deep partisan divisions, we wondered if we could offer a better description of those sentiments than just sticking party labels on them—we knew, coming out of the last election, that those labels can be too broad if there are differences among partisans in what they expected from the new administration, and that the single number of a president's job approval rating doesn't always capture the story, either. So we began a large study in which we described people by their expressed level of support or opposition to the new president, along with willingness to consider changing down the road, regardless of their party or ideology. We put together a big enough national sample to really dig into the subgroups, and we planned to reinterview people as the months went along so we could see specifically who changed, who didn't, and why. We wrote at the outset that through this lens, the president seemed to start with some potential, at least, for his support to vary up or down.

We separated the president's supporters into two types, the first of which were those who said they were "strong Trump supporter[s], period," and at the outset this group of backers made up a little over one in five Americans, at 22 percent. We described them as the "believers" for the thorough way in which, on item after item, they seemed to believe in the new president in terms of both his policies and his approach to the office. In that regard they differentiated themselves from other supporters who described their backing as more conditional. Almost all of these ardent backers felt he was doing things his own way or "shaking up" Washington, and were glad for it. Over time we would find that they listed, as big reasons for backing him, the feeling that he was "a different kind of president" taking on "the establishment" and speaking for people like them, which suggested a personal connection; one that would turn out to hold firm. Months later this group would still pick descriptions like these as reasons for their continued support, more so than that he had done things like cut their taxes. Over the course of our studies they also approved of what they saw in the president's political battles: they liked his tweeting relatively more than his conditional supporters did, and liked the fact that he seemed to be taking on political opponents, and making Democrats mad. They said they took the president's statements as a trusted source of information more than anything they got from the mainstream media. On policy, they overwhelmingly approved of building a border wall from the start, and as the term went on, a year into it, they continued to cite it and deportation of illegal immigrants as high policy priorities. We also saw how this group might not see themselves in terms of traditional polling tags: when asked to pick a party and ideology from the usual lists, many simply identified as conservative Republicans, and when asked how important each of these labels was to them: either that of Republican; or conservative; or Trump supporter, it was their identification as a Trump supporter that rated highest.

An additional set of supporters we called "conditional" made for another 22 percent of the country, and we described them as more transactional in their support for the president: they said they were backing him as long as he delivered on his promises. Compared to the stronger supporters, they were less enamored with his approaches to governance or communication such as tweets. They prioritized jobs and the economy over immigration at the outset of his term, and did think he was at least somewhat responsible for making the economy better as the term went on. As it turned out, this group would by and large stay with him.

Then there was a group who called themselves opponents at the moment, but said they might consider becoming supporters. They were 21 percent of Americans at the beginning of the term and we labeled them "curious" about whether the administration could deliver; they were the reason we thought his overall support levels did have some potential to increase, though that might not be easily done, and their decision-making criteria seemed to be in play. Half of them liked that he was shaking up Washington. Most said that he could earn at least some of their support if he made the economy better. But there was plenty of skepticism, too. Most also said he'd gain some support from them if they felt he showed respect for people of different views, and they differed with him on many issues. Eight in ten among them felt he was not showing respect at the start, but then, over time, even as the economy was seen as doing well in the minds of most Americans, this group did not become supporters.

Another 35 percent of the country said, at the start of his term, that they were firmly against Donald Trump, and across the measures they seemed just as steadfast in their stance as the staunchest supporters were in theirs. We labeled them the "resisters," opposed to his policies, and most said there wasn't anything they could foresee that could change their minds. This group was almost entirely made up of people who had not voted for him, or had not voted, and they described their feelings at the start as angry and pessimistic.

By the spring of 2018, and as discussion of the midterm elections built, two-thirds of Americans said the economy was in good shape and 68 percent gave the president's policies credit for that. The size of the president's strongest group of supporters stood at the same percentage it had been at the start of his term. Conditional supporters still were at similar levels, and those curious potential backers—those who said they might have considered supporting Donald Trump at the outset—were instead moving toward stronger opposition. The strongest opponent category of "resisters" had grown to 41 percent, rising from the 35 percent where it had started. We'd noted earlier that year that these Americans who gave him low marks had said they didn't feel he respected them and didn't like his personal behavior in office. It all described a slow hardening of opposition while that initial base held, but did not grow. We'd remember to keep an eye on the disparity in which positive views of the overall economy were not translating into growing support for the president—a theme that would echo later in the midterms.

I'd long felt that one lesson out of the 2016 presidential contest was that perhaps too many had made too much of the national poll numbers, which ultimately didn't decide the winner; it was the state races and the Electoral College that had mattered. And by the time we were getting set to poll the congressional races in the late spring of 2018, I'd also noted—in this book and elsewhere—that in a similar manner, the race for Congress is 435 separate races in the districts, yet many polls are still just national in scope, using that "generic ballot" to test one party against the other. So for the 2018 midterms, I figured I had to practice what I was preaching, and offer our viewers an actual House seat estimate—how many seats each party was getting out of 435.

We started with an extensive amount of survey data. We asked voters everywhere how they were voting, but then drew on another lesson from the previous election, which was to make sure to poll a lot where the action would likely be. In 2018 that meant the House races that we thought were closely contested, or that we thought could become so; where the parties were putting their money and advertising and had recruited strong candidates; and where the district profiles looked like there could be more potential new and swing voters. We reported what voters were thinking and feeling across these "battleground" districts that would collectively decide majority control, and leaned on them heavily to help us describe the overall picture.

Then for the actual seat estimates between Democrats and Republicans, the CBS News/ YouGov data science team combined the interview data on individuals' candidate choices into a model with district and national factors. This aimed to improve on the estimates for a district or subgroups in a district when the sample sizes were smaller than we'd have liked, by bringing in factors such as district demographics, past votes, and how many of each type of voter lived in the district. As we explained when the results were first released, using a technique called multilevel regression with post-stratification, it looked to get better estimates in any given district by learning from commonalities shared by voter groups across all of them, "so if we know a lot about, let's say, white working class voters, we can assume they have some commonalities, because opinions rarely stop at district or even state boundaries, especially as our politics becomes more nationalized. If we have a good estimate of this subgroup across the country, we can improve our estimate of the subgroup for any particular district." And then because politics is still partly local, too, it included district-specific factors such as whether a candidate running there was an incumbent, because we know that historically factors like that have an effect on results, as well. Finally, we took all the district estimates together and simulated the elections, and counted how many seats each party was winning. I've mentioned that pollsters often have to incorporate a lot of data and modeling beyond interviews these days, and our approach here continued in that vein.

Early in the summer of 2018, our first study found the Democrats were poised to gain seats and had a shot at the majority, if just barely at 219, which meant the contest for House control was starting as a toss-up—and one that subsequent estimates that summer and fall would show moving more toward a larger Democratic majority as voters increasingly made their decisions.

One voting break that emerged right away that summer was a large gender gap among all voters across the key congressional districts, with women backing Democrats, and men, Republicans. The intended vote split was especially pronounced among white women who held college degrees, who were breaking 52–32 for the Democratic candidates in their districts, while those without degrees were going for the Republican 42–35. Later in the summer women in the key districts gave the president a 57 percent disapproval rating on issues they felt affected women, with independent women at 53 percent disapproval. We also noted that agreement on health care policy was a top issue that women said was critical to a candidate earning their support. (It would later be paramount for all those voting Democratic nationwide.) And the partisan vote splits between college and noncollege voters would also be a hallmark of the election, and of the larger divides that have now emerged in the electorate—also a key one to watch in the next presidential race as well.

That summer when the immigration issue, family separations, and events at the southern border went to the forefront of the political debate, it defined some of the clearest differences we found between partisans, as well as between the president's supporters and opponents. His strongest backers were relatively more suspicious that at least some criminals were among the immigrants, and they were also more doubtful that the conditions reported in the detention centers were being accurately portrayed in the TV and news reports of the time. We asked, more generally, how those apprehended at the border ought to be treated. Nearly eight in ten Democrats said those entering the country illegally should be treated well, as an example of the nation's kindness, while three-fourths of Republicans said they needed to be punished, as an example of the nation's toughness on illegal activity. We also saw a difference in the issue's importance: 84 percent of Democrats, who overwhelmingly disapproved of the family separations, said the matter would be important to their upcoming congressional vote, almost twice the rate at which their Republican counterparts said so. Those who said they had never voted in a midterm before, but were planning to this time, said the events would steer their vote toward the Democrats—which at the time seemed an important factor given the Democrats' dependence on turning out less frequent voters.

In the fall of 2018, in those competitive congressional districts, we noted a large difference between the percent of people who said they were feeling good about the economy (75 percent) and those satisfied with the direction of the country overall (just 46 percent). This seemed like it pointed to a key voting group to watch. Historically, we thought, the good economy might have meant voters would give an edge to the party in power, the Republicans, but they were unhappy with the direction of the country, and that might pull them toward the party out of power, the Democrats. It turned out their negative views on the direction of the country took precedence. This group gave the president a low approval rating and most said that in their congressional vote they'd have considered a Republican who was more independent from Donald Trump, but fewer than one in five of them wanted a Republican congressperson who was in line with the White House. The women who were likely voters among them said by a wide margin they felt the Republicans were working against the interests of women.

Later that fall we'd ask voters in the swing districts what kind of factor the president would be, if any, in their choice for congressperson, and we found the number saying that he would be a factor headed for historically high levels of presidential influence. (On Election Day the national exit poll would bear this out. Sixty-four percent of voters said their congressional vote was at least partly to either express support for, or opposition to, the president, the largest number exit polls had measured about a president in recent midterms; higher than the number who said so about President George W. Bush when his party lost the House in 2006 or about President Barack Obama when his party was handed a lopsided congressional defeat in 2010. Within that group in 2018, those trying to send a message of opposition outnumbered supporters by 38 to 26, and their candidate choices went accordingly. It seemed, as we said at the time, that in House contests the president was not on the ballot, but he was on voters' minds.

• • •

By September we had the estimate at 224 seats for the Democrats, and in October we put the Democrats up with a majority 226 of 435 seats.

But I've emphasized the importance of looking for a range of possibilities in reporting poll information around campaigns. So in 2018, we wanted to make it even easier (I hoped) for folks to see things this way, and so we started offering scenarios for those House seat estimates: the high and low range of how many seats the Republicans and Democrats could get, depending on aspects of voters' *choices* that might reasonably change. This was more than just the margin of error. So, for instance, what might happen if voters on the fence about a party choice decided en masse to tilt one way or the other—as we know they can? What if people with irregular vote histories really did, or didn't, show up that year? We all know that actual turnout can certainly vary from what people tell us in pre-election polls. (I've increasingly seen other pollsters, too, putting out different estimate scenarios from their likely voter models in advance of races, and I think this is a welcome development. Some will invariably say it feels like a hedge, but, given what we know about uncertainty in estimates and the way people misinterpret them, and given that I think good pollsters are in the explanation business more so than the prediction one, I think being more explicit about the range of political possibilities is a good step.)

When we put out that October estimate of 226 for the Democrats, at the same time we offered a scenario showing what the race looked like if the infrequent voters and groups who were leaning Democratic actually turned out that year, as many were telling us they would. Modeling the expected number of House seats with that added potential turnout pushed the seat estimate all the way up to 235 for the Democrats. But then, we asked, what if those infrequent voters stayed home?—which one could also imagine happening, given their past voting histories. If that happened, we reported, it would mean Democrats would fall just short in their bid for the majority. Editorially, the three scenarios described an important political story about the dynamics of the race, showing the degree to which the Democrats' fortunes in their bid to retake the House were dependent on newer voters, and on reshaping the typical midterm electorate, particularly with—as we said at the time—"younger voters, non-whites, and college degree-holders" in the key districts.

In our final November study, we again offered scenarios for a range of what could happen. This time, just before Election Day, we had a baseline Democratic seats estimate of 225; then we described the conditions under which they'd fall short of a majority, if crossover voters went back to the Republicans; and then an estimate if there was high turnout and with crossover and independent voters choosing Democrats, for a high scenario of 232.

Election Day did in fact see record high turnout, with a jump of more than 30 million from the last midterm, boosted in part by people who had not taken part in a midterm before, and the Democrats got to 235 House seats. Exit polls showed that 16 percent of voters said it was their first time voting in a midterm, and these voters picked Democrats 62–36. In our pre-election polling, would-be voters' expressed intentions had been backed up by action, as 95 percent of the respondents who told us before the election that they would show up and vote then reported having done so. That included nearly all of those who'd described themselves as definitely going to vote, and three-quarters of those who'd only said that they "probably" would. We could also explain some of their motivation: in our final pre-election poll a quarter of voters in key House districts actually called the midterms more important than a presidential election—that included a lot of Democrats, eager for a chance to push back on Republican control—and another two-thirds said these races were just as important. On Election Day, Democratic House candidates did do relatively better in getting 2016 Donald Trump backers to cross and vote for them (8 percent) than Republican candidates did in drawing over Hillary Clinton voters (5 percent.) That crossover gap, though only in the single digits either way, was about what our pre-election estimates had suggested. Democrats also benefited from the late deciders this time around as the exit polls showed that in the last few days they went for the pre-election polling leader, the Democrats, by 53–41. All of it added up to us having the high range of our pre-election estimates for the Democrats coming closest to what emerged on Election Day.

It would actually take many days beyond Election Night to learn how close. The big story lines of House and Senate control were settled that night, but ballots were still being counted all over the country, and we didn't yet know the winners in more than a dozen congressional races and some important Senate and gubernatorial contests as well. Many of them were too close; many were in places out west that rely heavily on mail balloting, such as California, that can always take a while to tally all the votes. It was just that this year, with so many races so tight, the wait got more attention.

Republicans had clinched the Senate majority by picking up enough seats in places where they'd long been eyeing gains, like Indiana and North Dakota and Missouri, helped by the preponderance of Republican voters in those states—voters who strongly backed their party's candidates and denied Democrats much crossover—along with continued strong support in rural areas. Republicans were on their way to winning in Florida, too, while Arizona was still counting, and Democrats would ultimately get that.

The Democrats had won control of the House by picking up wins and flipping seats in an array of districts that ranged from wealthier to more working-class; from the East Coast and Mid-Atlantic, through the Midwest as the night had gone along, and a record number of women would be elected to Congress along the way. The question lingering on Wednesday morning was whether Democrats might also flip a string of suburban districts out in California. It was weeks before it all got sorted, but when they did, the results told a broader story not just about the size of the national Democratic House gain, but of a shifting electoral landscape in what had long been Republican territory.

In the meantime, though, I had gotten to leave before dawn.

The 2020 presidential primaries are approaching. Democratic hopefuls began announcing their bids to take on the incumbent president as early as the first months of 2019, and by the middle of 2019 we're starting the tough job of polling would-be primary voters. For poll watchers around that time, it's important to remember what those polls can show, and sometimes what they don't. They should describe the voters' mood, and good polls should define and differentiate the constituencies within a party, because those are the groups the campaigns are ultimately chasing. If you're thinking even farther ahead to the general election, pay attention to the differences between what those primary voters think is important—which issues, which policies—versus what voters overall think, because the former tend to be more ideological.

Early national "horse race" polls of nominee preferences don't, however, necessarily show you which candidate will end up ultimately winning those primaries, and that's not just because those polls start months in advance. Some candidates rise to the top of early polls because they're known names—which in the end may or may not help them politically, perhaps depending on whether voters come to want someone with more experience, or ultimately want someone newer to the scene. From an estimation standpoint, historically candidate positions and "leaders" in the primary polls shift around over time. You'll likely see many candidates separated by a mere point or two, which is well within sampling error; and the sub-samples of partisans within a national poll can be relatively smaller to begin with. We've done plenty of those polls over the years, just the same, and we went back and counted up seventeen different candidates who'd led or tied for a party's lead in those kinds of national CBS News polls across the last four presidential cycles. For a few examples, back in 2004 our polls on the Democratic side had candidates such as Howard Dean and Wesley Clark at the top at one point or another, though John Kerry eventually won the nomination; in 2007 before the 2008 primary contests Hillary Clinton led Barack Obama; and on the Republican side in 2012 we showed Rick Perry and Herman Cain, among others, vying for the top spot in a nomination fight that Mitt Romney would eventually win.

So it's better to watch polls that explain what voters are looking for and considering in the first place. Some polls will ask voters whether or not they would consider each one of the candidates, because voters might be mulling over more than one, and such polls will help show you the range of possibilities in the race, not just the leader at the moment. In a similar vein, some polls will measure whether voters have a favorable or unfavorable view of each candidate, which is also valuable information: candidates seen more favorably can have a better shot at moving into the consideration set if they aren't there already. Look for polls that explain how voters plan to ultimately make their choice: for instance, whether people are putting more weight on candidates' personal characteristics, or perceived electability—which isn't easy to judge, for anyone—or on policy differences.

The poll respondent picking a candidate early on also knows that the primaries are many months off, so their response to a simple horse race question early in the process might reasonably reflect a lot less consideration than it will months later, when their time to vote is really bearing down on them. Or a respondent may be using the time to consider many candidates in turn, before settling on one. And unless a respondent to a national poll lives in an early primary state, the whole race may be very different by the time they ever get to cast a ballot, anyhow: some candidates usually drop out after the early primaries, and some may emerge as more viable than others.

Then there's the pollster's task of identifying likely voters, which can be especially tough in primaries. The job of finding the would-be primary voter or caucus-goer gets harder because, despite the outsized attention these contests draw, far fewer people participate in them compared to general elections; the specific voters who do participate can vary a lot from cycle to cycle. A pollster might have to go back four or maybe eight years to find a historical comparison for past turnout—lots can change in a state in that time—and so a likely voter screen or model gets harder to do. We might need to make more assumptions about who and how to weight, and target, and that can open up more potential for inaccuracy. So when you see a primary poll, knowing who the likely voters are, and how the pollster defined them, becomes essential.

Politically, those voter preference polls aren't directly measuring what's at stake in the race, either. Primaries are contests for delegates to a party's national convention, and the states can vary in their rules for awarding those delegates, so pre-election polls offering just statewide vote percentages almost never translate straight into the number of delegates that each candidate would get. In the 2020 Democratic primaries, states will allocate some delegates proportionally to top finishers, and also by candidates' performance in its congressional districts. So simply knowing a polling leader or the top vote-getter doesn't tell the whole story when the second- and third-place finishers will get some delegates, too. That could be especially important in 2020 if a large field of candidates ends up splitting delegate hauls across many states.

Heading into this presidential campaign coming out of the 2018 midterms, though, the narrative about polling certainly felt positive. That was a

welcome difference from the way it had felt two years earlier. I was walking out to talk to an audience a couple of weeks after the midterm elections had wrapped up, and someone said aloud cheerfully, "Hey, I can
believe in the numbers again!" and I smiled. (Not to make too much of
it, but I liked the word "again," implying it was a return and not a new
discovery.) I knew some of the assessments were based on the elections
simply having gone as people generally expected, with the Republicans
winning the Senate and the Democrats, the House, and of course I have
cautioned against judging polls by just that criterion alone. But especially
for folks who had been doubtful, I was glad if they took it as evidence in
support of polling more generally. That sentiment was at least an easier
starting point for a conversation about what we pollsters try to do.

After those midterms we did another survey in which I asked people whether, regardless of what they'd wanted the outcome to be, they
thought the pre-election polls had generally been right or generally
wrong. I guess the good news is that by better than two to one, people
said they thought the midterm polls had been right (46 percent) more
than wrong (19 percent), while another third were not sure. For those
who said "right," I hoped at least part of the reason was that they felt the
polls had helped them understand the world a little bit better, too.

Acknowledgments

The number of people who have helped me along the way to this book seems too large even for this very lucky pollster to count. Here is a start.

This book exists in the first place because I'd keep running into Susan Zirinsky in the hallway in 2016 and would offer a casual "Oh, yeah, I'm going to write a book." Then she actually began the process to make it happen, first with her encouragement, and then putting me in touch with Jonathan Karp, who had the vision to make sure this project steered toward the future, not the past, as he wisely told me to try tackling bigger questions. Sean Manning, my editor, was so enormously patient as I juggled doing this with the other day job I had polling through 2017, and with his keen eye and gift for story he keeps me on the straight and narrow whenever I get too geeky. Most of the time, I listened. Fred Chase's copy edits were insightful and greatly improved many chapters, and Mark LaFlaur's guidance and patience were essential. And a deep thanks to Deneen Howell for her great guidance and support, and to Bob Barnett, fantastic agents both. I'm grateful to everyone on the Simon & Schuster team, to Emily Simonson for her organization and trying to keep me on deadline, to Jackie Seow for the cover art (and patience, too!), and to Cat Boyd.

I'm grateful to everyone at CBS News, and really lucky to work with such talented people where there are so many good ideas and so much passion for telling them. That starts with David Rhodes, endlessly innovative and supportive in this project in particular and in all our polling and election efforts. None of this—or our elections coverage—would be possible without Al Ortiz's constant support. I've never known anyone wiser, and I owe so much to his guidance. Ingrid Ciprian-Matthews's advice and guidance have always been essential and she has been so wonderfully supportive. I'm deeply grateful to Chris Isham for all the support for all things political and electoral, and to everyone along with him in the Washington bureau for all the insights and backing. And to Christa Robinson for the guidance and advice.

You know from the book that Kathy Frankovic hired me when I started here and basically set my life on an exciting and fulfilling course with that decision, for which I am eternally grateful—as well as for her reading early chapter drafts of this.

At around the same time, I met Murray Edelman, who taught me so many of the ideas I tried to relay here, how to look at things, how to make the data tell a story. Murray is one of the greats not just because of his skill with sampling and numbers but because he sees the human side of what we're measuring and what we're trying to communicate. I would simply not be here without him. But more than just being indebted, I remain endlessly admiring of his genius for solving polling and election puzzles and his desire to push the boundaries of what's possible even after he's already achieved so much. More particularly to this book, he's read draft upon draft, and made so many helpful comments, it wouldn't be the same without him.

I've been lucky to work over the years with the best of people, not just great pollsters. Sarah Dutton, the best friend and colleague a person could ask for, an award-winning pollster and simply one of the great people in the business, and who made many helpful comments on early chapter drafts. To the incredible Jen De Pinto, the consummate pro who never misses a detail, was kind enough to double-check me as she has a great knack for seeing ahead to topics and poll questions we need to be asking. Not only this book, but the whole CBS News poll is so much better for her efforts and insights. The endlessly talented Kabir Khanna who (as you can see from the references) brings such great data talent and number-crunching to a lot of the analyses we've done here and on elections, and is such a pleasure to work with; many of the insights I've presented here would not have been possible without his help. And the always creative Fred Backus, who also helped look over parts of this and whose insights, especially on trends over time, are always so valuable. There are so many CBS News poll questions, including many here from over the years that Sarah, Jen and Fred and Kabir, and Kathy, all had the foresight and skill to ask and analyze so well, and I am grateful for them.

Gary Moskowitz brilliantly makes all the elections systems work. Everything you see on Election Nights starts with his genius for computer systems, and especially the first chapter of this book—where we were able to review the data—was made possible by his development skills. Tim Hunter is the best at making everything look good on the graphics side and all that you see displayed and conveyed, and I'm very grateful to him, and Daniel Farray keeps us innovating relentlessly toward the twenty-second century. Linda Mason was always and still is a great source of support and guidance to whom I owe so much. And Jim Rosen, whose legacy of invention in those election systems lives on.

I am grateful to Doug Rivers for incredible innovations in the field and for the chance to work with him. Working with the great Delia Bailey is so much fun—and along with Eugenia Giraudy and everyone at YouGov America. Neither this book, nor much of our polling coverage in the last few years, would exist without them, their tireless and rigorous efforts, incredible volume of knowledge and care, and all the great data that produces. At SSRS, Eran Ben-Porath, Melissa Herrmann, and David Dutwin are such an incredible team in every respect, running a great operation and being great social scientists—a wonderful combination. They're all the best partners a pollster can have.

To the gang on the Decision Team—the best in the business, as far as I am concerned, and the people who put it all on the line on Election Nights. Mark Gersh is the guy with all the great insights and is always right. Our Decision Desk and our congressional coverage are so well served by his incredible talent all through the year, not just when the pressure is on in November. Doug, as mentioned; Steve Ansolabehere for his guidance and wisdom and all the great info, and for reading drafts of these chapters; David Winston for all the insights; and everyone who helped get through the hectic 2016 campaign and all those races: Brian Fraher, Martin Long, Joe Williams, Emily West, Bruce Willsie, Michael Myers, Tracy Deitz, and Nicole Sganga.

CBS News has such a wonderful team full of the best and most talented people I've known. For the folks at CBS who help get all the polls onto the air and online to our viewers and readers and listeners, and who go out and cover the people making the news and telling all those stories that are so important. I'm especially thankful to Mary Hager, always a big backer, and to John Dickerson for all the great conversations that helped hone the analyses all through the last election, and to the whole team at *Face the Nation*, who are amazing and the keenest analysts and editors. I'm deeply indebted to the great Bob Schieffer, always a terrific teacher, and who reminded us to keep focused on what people at home wanted to know. Great advice, indeed. To Nancy Lane and the whole gang at digital, for the strong support, creative vision, and search for new ideas; to Ryan Kadro and the gang at CTM; to Rob Gifford and the folks at CBSN digital and Red and Blue; Ellen Uchimya at cbsnews. com; Mosheh Oinounou and the gang at *Evening News*; Steve Capus; Jeff Fager; Jerry Cipriano; Andy Wolff, who read early drafts; Craig Swagler and everyone at radio; polling and election unit support from everyone who helps us tell the polling story with viewers and with whom I logged so many broadcasts and Election Nights over these years.

Friends and colleagues I've worked with on various polling and elections projects to help put together data, too, including Marjorie Connelly, Dalia Sussman, Megan Thee, Mike Kagay, John Broder, Janet Elder, Anni Robertson, Michael Butterworth, Marla Kaye, Gloria Price, Don Rehill, Rob Hendin, and Joe Lenski. To friends and family who've been supportive through the years, Dianna Stark, Jamie Stark, and Michael Weiss (who gave great advice at key times). Russ Dalton, who recruited me to grad school and introduced me to my wife, and Marty Wattenberg, Bernie Grofman, and everyone who taught me political science. Bert Molinari, who lent a hand with computers and moving vans back in the day. To Peter Crippen and the gang at Rex for encouragement and keeping me supplied with much-needed coffee.

And most of all, to my family.

To my wife, Lina Newton, who is a terrific scholar, and such a great mom, and I am so thankful for all her guidance and patience, especially when I hauled off on yet another weekend or late night to work on this. Lina is also a terrific editor, it turns out, and everyone knows she is a great political scientist, and is unsparing when things don't read well or are confusing—which I often badly needed to hear. She is totally awesome and I am very grateful. And to Aidan and Theo for making me laugh all the time, and who can finally stop asking when Daddy is going to finish his book. I would not have been able to do anything at all without all their backing. To my mom, who achieved so much and still found time to always be there for me; to my dad, who has always been there, and who is so supportive, and who backed me. So here's one final estimate, in which I am very confident: To them I owe more or less everything.

Notes

Chapter One: The Seen and the Unseen

7 *in this case, those first exit polls:* All descriptions here are of CBS News exit polls as conducted by Edison Media Research on behalf of the National Election Pool. As with any poll, exit polls need to account for sampling and possible nonresponse issues. For further reading on how exit polls are conducted and election results are estimated, see Warren Mitofsky and Murray Edelman, "Election Night Estimation," *Journal of Official Statistics* 18, no. 2 (2002): 165–79; Warren Mitofsky, "A Short History of Exit Polls," in *Polling and Presidential Election Coverage*, Paul Lavrakas and Jack Holley, eds. (Newbury Park, CA: Sage, 1991), 83–99; Daniel Merkle and Murray Edelman, "A Review of the 1996 Voter News Service Exit Polls from a Total Survey Error Perspective," in *Election Polls, the News Media, and Democracy*, Paul J. Lavrakas and Michael W. Traugott, eds. (New York: Chatham House, 2000).

11   *became a cornerstone of the modern approach:* Drawn from interviews with Murray Edelman conducted summer 2017 and from Mitofsky and Edelman, "Election Night Estimation," 165–79.

15   *We assume there are about 650,000 votes, and half of them are still uncounted:* County vote data in this chapter is drawn from the CBS News Election Night systems and our CBS News analyses and estimates at various times of the night. Vote counts in that system were sourced from the Associated Press. All exit poll data and reports are drawn from CBS News exit polls.

Chapter Two: Why Didn't You Call Me?

24   *the top one he'd gotten from the public for most of his career:* Sarah Igo, *The Averaged American* (Cambridge, MA: Harvard University Press, 2007). And see George Gallup, *The Pulse of Democracy* (New York: Simon & Schuster, 1940), 213–45, for discussion of skepticism.

25   *You get the idea:* Sources for population figures are U.S. Census Bureau estimates and computations based on past election results data and estimates from CBS News exit polls.

26   *when you aren't surveyed yourself:* Discussion of the idea of samples and representativeness can be found in Gallup, *The Pulse of Democracy*; and Carroll Glynn, Susan Herbst, Garrett J. O'Keefe, and Robert Shapiro, *Public Opinion* (Boulder, CO: Westview Press, 1999).

27   *their point of view might not be as popular:* See Ozan Kuru, Josh Pasek, and Michael W. Traugott, "Motivated Reasoning in the Perceived Credibility of Public Opinion Polls," *Public Opinion Quarterly* 81, no. 2 (May 30, 2017): 422–46.

30   *he compared sampling the country to tasting a "bowl of soup":* Gallup, *The Pulse of Democracy*, 56.

30   *oral traditions passed down through the family:* I'm going to use the word "sauce" here out of broader convention but my grandmother would have insisted that any red sauce with meat in it was always called "gravy."

Chapter Three: Finding You

37 *around 1,000 people to complete the survey:* Data is drawn from CBS News polls and SSRS, Inc. calculations.

38 *plenty of debate about that among pollsters initially:* For a review of the trends in survey research and the emergence of phones, see Michael J. Brick and Clyde Tucker, "Mitofsky–Waksberg: Learning from the Past," *Public Opinion Quarterly* 71, no. 5 (January 2007): 703–16, https://doi .org/10.1093/poq/nfm049; and Robert Groves, Paul Biemer, Lars Lyberg, James Massey, William Nichols, and Joseph Waksberg, *Telephone Survey Methodology* (New York: John Wiley & Sons, 1988). See also Warren Mitofsky, "Sampling of Telephone Households," unpublished CBS memorandum, 1970; Warren Mitofsky, "Presidential Address—Methods and Standards: A Challenge for Change," *Public Opinion Quarterly* 53, no. 3 (Jan. 1989): 446–53; and Joseph Waksberg, "Sampling Methods for Random Digit Dialing," *Journal of the American Statistical Association* 73, no. 361 (1978): 40–46.

39 *doesn't it matter much to you:* CBS News/*New York Times* poll, April 1977.

40 *on an exciting new venture in New York:* Interviews with Kathy Frankovic conducted summer 2017 and conversations from 2003 to 2008.

44 *simply declined more often when found:* Data is from the CBS News poll internal operations data and from the review literature on the decline of response rates in phone polls, which is extensive, e.g., Scott Keeter, "How Do We Know What We Know," in Paul Taylor, *The Next America* (New York: Perseus Books, 2014). As the change in rates effects on how telephone polling has changed as a result, see Robert M. Groves, "Three Eras of Survey Research," *Public Opinion Quarterly* 75, no. 5 (2011): 861–71; David Dutwin, "The Status of Telephone Interviewing in the U.S.," working paper posted at https://ssrs.com/status-telephone-interviewing-us/; Michael J. Battaglia, "Response Rates: How Have They Changed and Where Are They Headed?," in James Lepowski et al., *Advances in Telephone Survey Methodology*. See also Robert M. Groves, *Survey Errors and Survey Costs* (New York: John Wiley & Sons, 1989); and Paul

Lavrankas, *Telephone Survey Methods: Sampling, Selection and Supervision* (Newbury Park, CA: Sage Publications, 1987).

44 *even better than they'd been in 2012:* CBS News polls, October and November 2012.

44 *younger, often lower-income, and tight on time:* Anthony M. Salvanto, Eran Ben-Porath, and Kabir Khanna, working paper on household response rates, forthcoming.

45 *a process called weighting:* For a look at what response rates have done and implications for poll weighting, cell phones, their impact, and in comparison to other approaches, see Lavrankas, *Telephone Survey Methods*. Also see Scott Keeter, Courtney Kennedy, April Clark, Trevor Thompson, and Mike Mokrzycki, "What's Missing from National Landline RDD Surveys?: The Impact of the Growing Cell-Only Population," *Public Opinion Quarterly* 71, no. 5 (January 2007): 772–92, https://doi.org/10.1093/poq/nfm053; and Robert Groves, Don Dilman, John J. Eltinge, and Roderick J. A. Little., eds., *Survey Nonresponse* (New York: John Wiley & Sons, 2002).

46 *they may have ended up saving it:* See "Special Issue on Cell Phone Surveys," *Public Opinion Quarterly* 75, no. 2 (Summer 2011): 336–48.

47 *from what they used to be before them:* Based on the author's analysis of CBS News polls; and also see David Dutwin and Trent Buskirk, "Apples to Oranges or Gala Versus Golden Delicious?: Comparing Data Quality of Nonprobability Internet Samples to Low Response Rate Probability Samples," *Public Opinion Quarterly* 81, no. S1 (April 2017): 213–39.

50 *the polls could go wrong:* For discussion of the history of polling in this era, Kathleen Frankovic, Costas Panagopoulos, and Robert Y. Shapiro, "Opinion and Election Polls," in D. Pfeffermann and C. R. Rao, eds., *Handbook of Statistics—Sample Surveys: Design, Methods and Applications,* vol. 29A (The Netherlands: North-Holland, 2009): 567–96; and Carroll Glynn, Susan Herbst, Garrett J. O'Keefe, and Robert Shapiro, *Public Opinion* (Boulder, CO: Westview Press, 1999).

51 *one that they've continued since:* For more, see Stephen Ansolabehere and Douglas Rivers, "Cooperative Survey Research," *Annual Review of Political Science* 16, no. 1 (2013): 307–29; see also Schaffner, Brian F., and Stephen Ansolabehere, "Re-Examining the Validity of Different Survey

Modes for Measuring Public Opinion in the U.S.: Findings From a 2010 Multi-Mode Comparison," presented at the Annual Conference of the American Association of Public Opinion Research, Phoenix, AZ (May 2001), and the home page for the CCES at https://cces.gov.harvard.edu /publications?page=3.

52 *"all collected data using the Internet":* For review of the sample matching approach and use in surveys, see Ansolabehere and Rivers (ibid.); Lynn Vavreck and Douglas Rivers, "The 2006 Cooperative Congressional Election Study," *Journal of Elections, Public Opinion & Parties* 18, no. 4 (208): 355–66; and Doug Rivers and Delia Bailey, "Inference from Matched Samples in the 2008 U.S. National Elections," American Association of Public Opinion Research, *Journal of Survey Methodology* (2009).

53 *up dramatically from just 35 percent in 2011:* Pew Research Center, *Americans' Internet Access, 2000–2015,* June 26, 2015, http://www.pewinternet .org/2015/06/26/americans-internet-access-2000-2015/.

Chapter Four: How to Avoid Surprises

58 *Reluctant Republicans were about 10 percent:* CBS News Battleground Tracker polls, July and August 2016, September and October 2016.

59 *that there was a deficit within his party: Face the Nation* transcript, August 21, 2016, https://www.cbsnews.com/news/face-the-nation-transcript-august -21-2016-priebus-sessions-mook/. For an example of on-air descriptions, see *CBS This Morning,* October 25, 2017.

59 *Election Day to our last pre-election poll there:* This analysis compares estimates from pre-election polls in the 2016 CBS News Battleground Tracker series to 2016 CBS News Exit Polls.

60 *and that may have been most telling of all:* Some said they were voting for a third party, but we know historically that tends to trail off. See Joe Lenski, "Evaluation of Methods for Polling Third Party Candidates," presentation at AAPOR National Conference, May 13, 2016.

61 *if they haven't come around to supporting it by Election Day:* This analysis covers CBS News 2016 exit polls.

62 *to sound politically correct:* Andrew Kohut, "Getting It Wrong," *New York*

Times, January 10, 2008. Also note that our own CBS News poll released in advance of the New Hampshire primary had, however, also stated the race was still very fluid heading into the final days. That part turned out to be right.

62 *it wasn't a dramatic difference:* There's also the view that measuring these effects, if any, could also be confounded by white respondents refusing African American interviewers at a higher rate in the first place, which would in turn reduce the percentage of white respondents who did not provide accurate responses when interviewed. For discussion of race of interviewer effects, see Howard Schulman and Jean M. Converse, "The Effects of Black and White Interviewers on Black Responses in 1968," *Public Opinion Quarterly* 35, no. 1 (January 1, 1971): 44–68; and Steven E. Finkel, Thomas M. Guterbock, and Marian J. Borg, "Race of Interviewer Effects in a Pre-election Poll: Virginia 1989," *Public Opinion Quarterly* 55, no. 3 (Autumn 1991): 313–30.

63 *and the economy still sluggish:* Noam Scheiber, "The Internal Polls That Made Mitt Romney Think He'd Win," *The New Republic*, November 30, 2012.

64 *a lot of shyness on their part:* More generally, as the campaign wore on and it was obvious to any Trump voter that at least 45 percent of the country—millions of Americans—agreed with them, it gets harder to see how saying they supported him was undesirable.

64 *lying is really hard work:* Kathy Frankovic, "To Tell the Truth to Pollsters," CBSNews.com, August 15, 2007, https://www.cbsnews.com/news/to-tell-the-truth-to-pollsters/.

66 *Trump was better than Clinton:* Analysis of CBS News polls and CBS News Battleground Tracker polls, summer and fall 2016.

67 *But these voters aren't always opposed to polls:* Andrew Gelman, Sharad Goel, Douglas Rivers, and David Rothschild, "The Mythical Swing Voter," working paper, http://www.stat.columbia.edu/~gelman/research/unpublished/swing_voters.pdf. Also see Doug Rivers, "Beware the Phantom Swings," working paper, https://today.yougov.com/news/2016/11/01/beware-phantom-swings-why-dramatic-swings-in-the-p/, in which he studied YouGov America polls that looked at response rates and found

that "although we didn't find much vote switching, we did notice a different type of change: the willingness of Clinton and Trump supporters to participate in our polls varied by a significant amount depending upon what was happening at the time of the poll."

67 *if we'd really gauged their likelihood:* This analysis is the result of data from an internal 2016 YouGov America Post-Election recontact study and shared with the author via personal communication.

69 *African American voters declined:* Thomas File, U.S. Census, *Social, Economic and Housing Statistics Division Voting in America: A Look at the 2016 Presidential Election,* May 10, 2017.

69 *and over one-third of them black:* Philip Bump, "4.4 Million 2012 Obama Voters Stayed Home in 2016—More than a Third of Them Black," *Washington Post,* March 12, 2018, https://www.washingtonpost.com/amphtml /news/politics/wp/2018/03/12/4-4-million-2012-obama-voters-stayed -home-in-2016-more-than-a-third-of-them-black. The *Post* also notes that social media efforts from the Russian trolls had had the goal of trying to suppress African American turnout.

The turnout study cited appeared in Sean McElwee, Jesse H. Rhodes, Brian F. Schaffner, and Bernard L. Fraga, "The Missing Obama Millions," *New York Times,* March 10, 2018, https://www.nytimes.com/2018/03/10 /opinion/sunday/obama-trump-voters-democrats.html. Poll findings from CBS Battleground Tracker, July 2016, and CBS News Poll, December 2017.

70 *every county in America:* Doug Rivers, "What the Hell Happened?," presentation, Stanford University, April 24, 2017, provided to the author by Rivers. Rivers's study is cited in David Leonhardt, "The Democrats' Real Turnout Problem," *New York Times,* November 17, 2017, https://www.nytimes.com/2016/11/20/opinion/sunday/the-democrats -real-turnout-problem.html. Also in this study, Rivers showed that in Pennsylvania, counties Obama had lost big showed close to ten-point jumps in turnout in 2016. In Michigan, the heavy Republican counties from 2012 showed greater than eight-point turnout jumps, while turnout was down two points in Democratic places, where Obama had won with more than 65 percent four years prior. Ohio was really dramatic—as we saw when we called it—with turnout dropping over four points in

dominantly Democratic places and jumping, on average, across all the Republican ones. Even in places where both parties managed turnout spikes, the Republicans bested the Democrats on their sizes.

71 *A study by a team of political scientists:* Andrew Guess, Brendan Nyhan, and Jason Reifler, "You're Fake News!," Poynter media trust survey, November 2017, poyntercdn.blob.core.windows.net, http://www.dart mouth.edu/~nyhan/fake-news-2016.pdf.

72 *American Association of Public Opinion Research:* For more on the 2016 polls and post-election analysis, and on the late shifts, see "An Evaluation of 2016 Election Polls in the U.S.," American Association for Public Opinion Research Ad Hoc Committee on 2016 Election Polling, http://www.aapor.org/Education-Resources/Reports/An-Evaluation -of-2016-Election-Polls-in-the-U-S.aspx. Also see Scott Clement, "The 2016 National Polls Are Looking Less Wrong After Final Election Tallies," *Washington Post,* January 13, 2017.

72 *Trump in Ohio and Florida the final weekend:* CBS News Ohio and Florida Battleground Tracker surveys, November 2016.

72 *And in the future you'll probably see:* For example, techniques such as Multilevel Regression with Poststratification are gaining favor. See Ben Lauderdale, "The YouGov Model: The State of the 2016 Election," https:// today.yougov.com/news/2016/10/04/YouGov-Model-State-of-2016/; and Andrew Gelman, "The Polls of the Future Are Reproducible and Open Source," *Slate,* December 29, 2017, http://www.slate.com/articles /technology/future_tense/2016/11/the_polls_of_the_future_will_be_re producible_and_open_source.html.

Chapter Five: What Are You Trying to Say?

75 *It's balanced:* If we do ask Mike to answer what we call an open-ended question, as in, "How are you?," we need to apply a judgment to all the descriptions we might get from him and everyone else. Mike might sound happy and say "I'm good," but then when Barbara comes along, and we ask her, she might describe things as "cool." Or "I'm all right." Is that the same as Mike's "I'm good"? Figuring that out is time-consuming

and leaves room for error—error that would come from us not classifying everything the way the respondents meant it. So we usually standardize things and let people sort themselves. Open-ended questions are better used sparingly, for times when the list would be far too long for us to come up with, but the answers will probably be short: "What do you think is the most important problem facing the country today?" is one of our longest-running examples. A lot of the time—in good times and bad—people just say, "The economy."

75   *"poll" comes from the Middle English: Merriam Webster Dictionary Online,* https://www.merriam-webster.com/dictionary/pollC; and *Collins Diction-ary,* https://www.collinsdictionary.com/word-lovers-blog/new/we-take-a-look-at-the-etymology-behind-the-word-poll,293,HCB.html.

79   *Some of those responses were driven:* Answers to these questions can be motivated by a person's desire to voice support for their party more generally, or to fall back on a shortcut that whatever their party is doing is probably the right thing, at least more generally.

80   *or if they're even in the market for a car:* Norman Bradburn, Seymour Sudman, and Brian Wansink, *Asking Questions* (San Francisco: John Wiley & Sons, 2004).

81   *"condemning Mr. Trump for divisiveness":* Ken Belson, "Fueled by Trump's Tweets, Anthem Protests Grow to a Nationwide Rebuke," *New York Times,* September 24, 2017.

82   *neither the kneeling nor the president's involvement:* This analysis covers CBS News/YouGov Poll, September 2017.

83   *I asked:* "Whether or not you agree with them": CBS News Nation Tracker poll, September 2017.

Chapter Six: What's the Story?

85   *asked about that in October 2011:* The full text of the question was "Do you believe in ghosts, or that the spirits of dead people can come back in certain places or situations?" CBS News poll October 2011.

86   *Even her detractors in the polling:* CBS News Battleground Tracker polls, 2016.

87 *Not for their sake, but for yours:* CBS News Battleground Tracker poll, fall 2017.

87 *and a third of them called it a crisis:* CBS News poll, August 2017.

88 *guns one of the country's biggest problems:* This analysis is derived from CBS News/YouGov poll, December 2017.

92 *Mental health screenings and treatment initiatives:* CBS News polls, December 2017 and February 2018.

Chapter Seven: How to Learn a Lot from a Little

95 *You look at one of those review websites where moviegoers:* These movies and ratings are fictional, and I must credit my publisher Jonathan Karp for the playful title of *The Pollster Always Rings Twice.*

97 *makes us more confident in our description of it:* This is the idea of a distribution, that the spread of a set of data can tell you more about what it's describing than just its average alone.

104 *Do you feel . . . confident?:* Okay, well, some of my colleagues note that this analogy doesn't really square with the idea that if you're doing a poll, you already must have a bullet—i.e., that you have something that will potentially land in the right range. This is a fair point. I like to use it mainly to get people thinking about the idea of certainty and uncertainty. What I'm working toward here is the idea of a confidence interval.

104 *95 out of 100 times if we repeated the poll:* This is based on an idea called a confidence interval. See Jerzy Neyman, "On the Two Different Aspects of the Representative Method: The Method of Stratified Sampling and the Method of Purposive Selection," *Journal of the Royal Statistical Association* 97 (1934): 558–625; for general work on probability, see Ian Hacking, *The Emergence of Probability* (Cambridge, UK: Cambridge University Press, 1975); for applications in surveys, see Robert Groves, Paul Biemer, Lars Lyberg, James Massey, William Nichols, and Joseph Waksberg, *Telephone Survey Methodology* (New York: John Wiley & Sons, 1988); and for a discussion of election polls, see Paul Lavrakas, Michael Traugott, and Peter V. Miller, *Presidential Polls and the News Media* (Boulder, CO: Westview Press, 1991).

105   *But no matter how good you get, no one is perfect:* If you do want to understand how smaller segments of the population think, though, then you
might need either targeted or larger samples, up around 1,500 or 2,000
or more, because margins of error for estimates in sub-samples—any particular groups within the poll, such as young people, older people, whites,
blacks—will be larger than for the whole poll sample because you're ana-
lyzing a smaller fraction of the whole.

    The margin of error is a theoretical idea and, given the stresses of
polling now, with lower response rates and harder-to-reach people, it gets
us farther from the pure ideal. There isn't any poll I know of—phone,
online, or otherwise—that perfectly draws a true random sample of the
population of the sort I've described in my examples, given all the logis-
tical difficulties of finding people today. These are ideals, and ways of
comparing estimates across different polls.

106   *A sample of 1,000 . . . is not magical:* The idea of margin of error also has
to be approached differently for a poll that isn't trying to be a probability
sample—that is, one that doesn't proceed from the premise that it could
randomly pull respondents from among everyone in the country. This
happens with a lot of polls that assemble representative samples from
panels online. There, we typically look at how much variance, or spread,
there is within the data that we collect in any given poll. We figure out
what would happen if, given that spread, we repeated the poll again and
again; that is, how likely it would be that we'd come up with something
around the same number again. Here we're making use of the same idea
that repetition can show us how certain we ought to be about any given
poll estimate we produce. However, if different organizations approach
their calculations a little differently, that can make it harder to directly
compare the possible error in estimates between different polls.

106   *a CBS News poll released in 2015:* CBS News poll, May 2015.

107   *CBS News national poll from August 2012:* We do as is customary in the
industry: report the margin of error for the whole poll. Technically parameters closer to the 0 and 100 have lower theoretical MOEs. Technically the margin would be smaller here. MOEs for a poll are computed
for parameters at 50 percent, where they have the most room to vary to

either side between 0 and 100. I take a bit of license in this example and use the three points anyway to stay consistent with the way polls are typically reported to the viewer.

Chapter Eight: You Be the Judge

109 *By some traditional measures:* U.S. Bureau of Labor statistics.

109 *percentage of Americans who said:* CBS News polls, October 2016; December 2016; January 2017; February 2017.

111 *point out how well polling generally works:* In their classic study *The Rational Public*, Ben Page and Robert Shapiro went through decades' worth of polling and found "collective policy preferences are generally stable; they change in understandable, predictable ways." Ben Page and Robert Shapiro, *The Rational Public* (Chicago: University of Chicago Press, 1992).

112 *Pollsters have been charting partisan splits:* See Andrew Kohut, "Resurgent Public Optimism on the Economy? Don't Hold Your Breath," Pew Research Center report, March 17, 2014, http://www.pewresearch.org /fact-tank/2014/03/17/resurgent-public-optimism-on-the-economy -dont-hold-your-breath/. Also, political scientists found that Democrats' views of the economy improved after their party took over Congress and discuss the larger phenomenon of evaluations in Allen Gerber and Greg Huber, "Partisanship, Political Control, and Economic Assessments," *American Journal of Political Science* 54, no. 1 (January 2010).

112 *how-are-things-style questions:* For a discussion of one of the classic studies of how people make decisions about the economy, including who uses their own personal situation and who tries to gauge the larger context, see Angus Campbell, Philip E. Converse, Warren E. Miller, and Donald E. Stokes, *The American Voter* (Chicago: University of Chicago Press, 1980); and Warren Miller and J. Merrill Shanks, *The New American Voter* (Cambridge, MA: Harvard University Press, 1996).

113 *implications, costs, and consequences:* These aren't the only factors. Whether or not there is a clear right answer, political and social science has noted that these poll responses might be a chance for the respondent to voice indirect support for their side, their partisan team, or a chance to knock the

opposing one, which can have emotional benefits. It might be that people are being exposed to information that's positive or negative, if they're listening to news with more partisan slants. They might be answering the survey with that recent information in their heads. There might be connections between the economic fortunes and whatever brought them to the partisanship they hold in the first place. All that doesn't make their answers invalid, though, but it changes how we can interpret their thinking and how they arrive at it. Some readings, for example: John Zaller, *The Nature and Origins of Mass Opinion* (New York: Cambridge University Press, 1992); and Donald Green, Bradley Palmquist, and Eric Schickler, *Partisan Hearts and Minds: Political Parties and the Social Identities of Voters* (New Haven, CT: Yale University Press, 2002). And this is hardly the only measure on which it happens. In our own CBS News polls the approval ratings gaps between how Republicans have rated a Democratic president, and how Democrats rated a Republican president, have also grown in recent decades. In early 2017—before a large section of ISIS territory fell that summer—we asked people how the fight against ISIS was going, and we asked it the exact same way as we had before Donald Trump took office. To Republicans, things on the battlefield had gotten better in a hurry. Just 16 percent of Republicans said the fight was going well in September 2016. By the spring, 72 percent said it was going well, a 56-point increase. Some important things did happen militarily in between, but the biggest explanation why *one* party might see such a jump is again obvious: a political change. Data in this section is from CBS News and CBS News/*New York Times* polls, 1980s–present. On health care: CBS News polls taken September 2009, March 2010, July 2010, January 2011, and March and September 2017; on marriage, CBS News polls taken February 2004, March 2013, and October 2016.

113   *evaluate it with different measures in the first place:* There is extensive work—and debate—in political science over the extent to which people use shortcuts in processing political information and evaluating policy, and how partisans use partisanship to make sense of the world. There is also the possible desire to voice support for their partisan team in surveys, and the emotional benefits that it might also bring. There is evidence

that partisanship affects factual beliefs. See John G. Bullock, Alan S. Gerber, Seth J. Hill, and Gregory A. Huber, "Partisan Bias in Factual Beliefs About Politics," *Quarterly Journal of Political Science* 10 (2015): 519–78. One introduction to voters and the use of shortcuts overall can be found in Samuel Popkin, *The Reasoning Voter: Communication and Persuasion in Presidential Campaigns* (Chicago: University of Chicago Press, 1991). Also see Arthur Lupia, *Uninformed: Why People Seem to Know So Little about Politics and What We Can Do about It* (New York: Oxford University Press, 2016).

113 *simply say what you want to be the case:* Princeton political scientists conducted an experiment in which they gave people incentives to answer factual economic conditions correctly—something a public poll would never do—to try to tease out respondents who really did know more than their partisan-tinged answers might suggest. Some respondents did not know those facts, and so simply filled in the gaps with partisan-fueled assumptions—in other words, they didn't know how the economy was, but did know the other party was in charge, so things must therefore be bad. And others were using the poll as a chance to feel like they were supporting their party, or to give views of "what they would like to be true." See Markus Prior, Gaurav Sood, and Kabir Khanna, "You Cannot Be Serious: The Impact of Accuracy Incentives on Partisan Bias in Reports of Economic Perceptions," *Quarterly Journal of Political Science* 10, no. 4 (2015): 489–518.

113 *the source looking out for their interests:* The more knowledge a voter has, the more likely he or she is to have opinions. See Delli Carpini, Michael X, and Scott Keeter, *What Americans Know About Politics and Why It Matters* (New Haven, CT: Yale University Press, 1996).

114 *They got different answers:* CNBC AAES Third Quarter Survey, September 2013, by Hart Research/Pubic Opinion Strategies; and see Steve Liesman, "What's in a Name? A Lot When It Comes to Obamacare," CNBC .com, https://www.cnbc.com/2013/09/26/whats-in-a-name-lots-when-it-comes-to-obamacareaca.html.

114 *decoding something that they're not otherwise very familiar with:* The literature on knowledge and confirmation biases and motivating reasoning is

long. One example is Charles S. Taber and Milton Lodge, "Motivated Skepticism in the Evaluation of Political Beliefs," *American Journal of Political Science* 50, no. 3 (July 2006): 755–69.

116 *went from having one in twenty people as foreign-born to:* Elizabeth Griego, U.S. Census report, "The 'Second Great Wave' of Immigration: Growth of the Foreign-Born Population Since 1970," February 26, 2014, https:// www.census.gov/newsroom/blogs/random-samplings/2014/02/the -second-great-wave-of-immigration-growth-of-the-foreign-born-popula tion-since-1970.html.

116 *Paul Taylor describes demographic transformation:* Paul Taylor, *The Next America* (New York: Perseus Books, 2014), 31.

117 *more likely to say immigration contributes to the nation:* CBS News Nation Tracker, 2017.

117 *Ron Brownstein, whose studies look:* Ron Brownstein, "America a Year Later," CNN.com, November 6, 2017, http://www.cnn.com/interactive /2017/politics/state/2016-election-anniversary/.

117 *jobs available today than they had in the 1960s:* Ron Brownstein, "Brown, Grey and Urban," *The Atlantic*, April 24, 2015, https://www.theatlantic .com/politics/archive/2015/04/brown-gray-and-urban/431964/.

118 *By 2015 Americans were twice as likely:* CBS News polls, 2018.

118 *a Pew study in 2018 found:* Samantha Neal, Pew Research Center report, "Most Americans View Openness to Foreigners as 'Essential to Who We Are as a Nation,'" August 4, 2017.

118 *Those two perceptions were linked:* Data from CBS News Nation Tracker, September 2017.

119 *In 2017, over half of Republicans were in favor:* CBS News poll, January 2017.

119 *especially high on such sentiment:* Although the Trump campaign seized on the issue, this was not simply a 2016 phenomenon. In 2012, Republican primary voters were also opposed to offering paths to citizenship. In the run-up to the 2008 Republican South Carolina primary, our poll found that immigration was the number one issue, and in the Florida primary, four in ten favored deportation. CBS News Florida Primary Exit Poll, 2008.

119 *Immigration was not the top:* Data in this section is from CBS News exit polls, 2016 Republican primaries, winter-spring 2016.

120 *Differences between Republicans generally:* Comparison of CBS News poll, January 2016, and CBS News exit polls, 2016 Republican primaries.

120 *stood out in their opposition to immigration:* CBS News Nation Tracker, February 2017 and January 2018.

120 *there was wide favor among Republicans for allowing some form of legalization:* CBS News poll, December 2017.

120 *as African American Democrats tend to have:* CBS News Nation Tracker, September 2017, and 2017 CBS News/YouGov Nation Tracker surveys.

Chapter Nine: It All Comes Down to Turnout

123 *We asked people who said they didn't always vote:* These and referenced reasons for not turning out are from the CBS News/YouGov Generations and Activism Study, March 2018.

123 *we asked people how they'd felt watching all the events unfold:* CBS News/ YouGov Generations and Activism Study, March 2018.

124 *lowly 36 percent in 2014*: All turnout data here is from turnout scholar Michael McDonald, United States Elections Project, http://www.elect project.org/. Also see U.S. Census Bureau voting and registration reports.https://thedataweb.rm.census.gov/TheDataWeb_HotReport2 /voting/voting.hrml?GESTFIPS=51&INSTANCE=Nov+2016. See also Giovanni Russonello, "When It Comes to Voting, Minnesota Makes It Easy," *The New York Times*, November 4, 2016: https://www.nytimes .com/2016/11/05/us/politics/voter-turnout-minnesota.html, and Michael McDonald's "America Goes to the Polls: A Report on Voter Turnout": https://www.nonprofitvote.org/america-goes-to-the-polls-2016/.

126 *eight in ten registered voters vote in presidential elections:* Based on CBS News recontact surveys, CBS News analysis of L2 voter files, and U.S. Census, American Community Survey, Voter Turnout.

128 *We want to avoid people saying they're paying more attention:* Attention is not a perfect predictor. It can under-predict a vote, too: someone might be a hard partisan and know exactly who they'll vote for the moment

their party's nominee is announced, and be certain that they'll vote, and therefore they'll see no need at all to pay attention to the twists of the campaign.

128   *was still more than 24 percentage points lower:* Thomas File, U.S. Census, "Social, Economic and Housing Statistics Division Voting in America: A Look at the 2016 Presidential Election," May 10, 2017.

128   *long-running study of young voters led by pollster John Della Volpe:* Spring 2017 Millennials Poll, Harvard Institute of Politics, http://iop.harvard .edu/youth-poll/harvard-iop-spring-17-poll.

129   *People vote when they think:* Turnout is more than just a challenge for pollsters, it's been a core concern of political science. For reading and exploration of all these, and other factors influencing the vote, see Frances Fox Piven and Richard Cloward, *Why Americans Don't Vote* (New York: Pantheon, 1988); Martin Wattenberg, *Where Have All the Voters Gone?* (Cambridge, MA: Harvard University Press, 2002).

129   *Some pollsters try to figure out:* Voters do tend to have more resources than nonvoters in terms of money, time, and information. Money can buy time, maybe time to hire a babysitter while you go vote, or maybe the flexibility to forgo an offered hour of overtime in order to go vote. Maybe someone has an office job and won't be penalized for walking in a bit late if the voting lines are long, versus someone who has a shift job and needs to get in exactly on time or they're in trouble. Or maybe if the courthouse or place to go register or get an ID is far away and it requires a car to get there, whether or not you have a car can make all the difference.

Time is a resource for all of us, and voting takes time, if not to stand in line, then to drop off an early ballot, or fill out your absentee request, or perhaps just to watch enough of the campaign that you feel like you're making an informed decision. Political participation more generally takes not just knowledge but civic skills. Voters need to know where their polling place or vote center is, where to go and which forms to ask for, and how to navigate those forms.

There was a time when some scholars thought it didn't make much sense for anyone to vote unless they thought the race was so tight they could cast the deciding ballot, but it turns out other feelings can also be thought of as emotional or psychological benefits that people want, like feeling that you're being a good citizen, supporting the national party, participating in a communal act.

129 *Campaigns increasingly target voters using information:* See Sasha Issenberg, *The Victory Lab* (New York: Broadway Books, 2012). Also see Kristen Soltis Anderson, *The Selfie Vote: Where Millennials Are Leading America* (New York: Broadside Books, 2014).

131 *information is by and large publicly available:* For more on voter lists, see Steve Ansolabehere and Eitan Hirsh, "Validation: What Big Data Reveal About Survey Misreporting and the Real Electorate," in *Political Analysis*, 2012, http://pan.oxfordjournals.org/content/early/2012/08/27/pan .mps023.short.

133 *population that really does show up to vote:* Different polls apply these weights and scores differently. Different polls might use different combinations of these factors depending on the race or the year. For more on a review of what different polls do differently, see Scott Keeter and Ruth Igielnik, "Measuring the Likely Voter," Pew Research Center report, January 2016, http://www.pewresearch.org/2016/01/07/measuring-the -likelihood-to-vote/.

134 *especially true in the midterm elections, like 2014:* Some of this is because there isn't a presidential race to grab everyone's attention, and some of it is idiosyncratic because high-intensity, competitive Senate races don't always take place in the high-population states like New York and California and Florida.

135 *just 2 percent of initial Democrats:* Anthony Salvanto and Kabir Khanna, CBS News partisanship study, cbsnews.com, September 14, 2017.

135 *half of all independents who went to the polls:* CBS News 2016 National exit polls.

136 *half of them said they picked a single party:* For example, CBS news polls, January 2016. Regarding the comparison of independent numbers, also note that the polls do ask the question a little differently, with the exit poll offering independent or something else, and the CBS News national poll placing those who don't know in the independent category as well.

136 *"more likely than those in older generations to call themselves independents":*

Pew Research Center report, "Trends in Party Affiliation Among Demographic Groups," March 20, 2018, http://www.people-press.org/2018/03/20/1-trends-in-party-affiliation-among-demographic-groups/.

136 *millennials are not following the old models:* Anderson, *The Selfie Vote,* chapter 1.

Chapter Ten: Counting on Congress

138 *Looking back through our records from the Desk:* CBS News House model and competitive district ratings, 2002–2016.

138 *In the 1990s it wasn't unusual to find congressional approval:* CBS News polls, 1990–2000.

139 *a mere 6 percent of contests have seen a party turnover:* Data from CBS News Election Unit counts of congressional results, 2002–2016. We're hardly alone in pointing out the low rate of turnover, it's a long-standing point in American politics. See "Vital Statistics on Congress," Brookings Institution report, September 7, 2017, https://www.brookings.edu/multi-chapter-report/vital-statistics-on-congress/; and Drew Desilver, Pew Research Center, "House Seats Rarely Flip," http://www.pewresearch.org/fact-tank/2016/09/07/house-seats-rarely-flip-from-one-party-to-the-other/.

139 *only one-third could name theirs:* Gallup Organization, Gallup Poll, May 2013, Cornell University, Ithaca, New York, Roper Center for Public Opinion Research, iPOLL [distributor], accessed February 13, 2018; Data from the CBS study is from CBS News Nation Tracker poll, March 2018.

140 *Ninety-four percent of incumbents who sought reelection won it:* CBS News Election Unit records, 2000–2016.

141 *are sticking more and more to their:* Christopher Hare, Keith T. Poole, and Howard Rosenthal, "Polarization in Congress Has Risen Sharply; Where Is It Going Next?," *Washington Post,* February 13, 2014; and Keith T. Poole and Howard Rosenthal, *Congress: A Political-Economic History of Roll Call Voting* (Oxford: Oxford University Press, 1997).

141 *and almost as many Democrats crossed back:* Source is national exit polls, 1984–2014. Some of this is a function of a bygone era when longtime

incumbents drew those votes across party lines, especially long-serving Democrats who were still holding office throughout the South while the region was otherwise trending toward the Republicans.

141 *When an incumbent steps aside:* Data is from an internal CBS News February 2018 analysis of past House votes.

142 *have one question that everyone in the country answers:* There's no sense in inserting the names of local congresspersons because the poll is a national sample, and it wouldn't be able to estimate any one district, anyway.

Chapter Eleven: Is It Really a Horse Race?

147 *top name in some vote-choice polls:* See for example the *Washington Post/ABC News* poll, December 2014.

147 *candidates we gave people and asked:* CBS News polls, 2014–2015.

148 *lowest favorable rating of any front-runner we'd measured:* CBS News polls, July–October 2016.

148 *said they'd consider switching their vote to Trump:* Analysis of CBS News polls and CBS News Battleground Tracker polls, summer and fall 2016.

149 *easier than getting a basketball team to the Final Four:* Steven Shepard, "The Poll That Built a University," *Politico Magazine*, December 12, 2017, https://www.politico.com/magazine/story/2017/12/12/quinnipiac -poll-university-history-216066.

149 *RealClear Politics.com's listing from May to November 2016:* www.real clearpolitics.com poll listings, https://www.realclearpolitics.com/epolls /2016/president/us/general_election_trump_vs_clinton-5491.html.Retrieved January 2018.

149 *total number of public polls of any sort:* Benjamin Toff, "The 'Nate Silver Effect' on Political Journalism: Gatecrashers, Gatekeepers, and Changing Newsroom Practices Around Coverage of Public Opinion Polls," *Sage Journals*, September 15, 2017.

149 *"logged 1,240 state-level polls":* Mark Blumenthal, "Polls, Forecasts and Aggregators," in *PS: Political Science and Politics*, American Political Science Association, April 2014.

150 *a couple from Colorado or Ohio:* RealClearpolitics.com listings, https://

www.realclearpolitics.com/epolls/2016/president/us/general_election
_trump_vs_cl.inton-5491.html. Retrieved January 2018.

150 *These aggregator websites draw millions:* Toff, "The 'Nate Silver Effect' on Political Journalism."

151 *Blumenthal's study counted the Google searches:* Blumenthal, "Polls, Forecasts and Aggregators."

153 *I've used the following example talking to our producers:* It's a newsroom-centric riff on an old parable passed down from John Venn in Stephen Stigler's *The Seven Pillars of Statistical Wisdom* as he shares a story of a sea captain who needed to know what size cannonballs to use, got different answers, and was unable to average them because there was only one correct size cannonball. Stephen M. Stigler, *The Seven Pillars of Statistical Wisdom* (Cambridge, MA: Harvard University Press, 2016), 58. A few of us pollsters have our own different versions of the idea. In Bob Schieffer' (Bob Schieffer with H. Andrew Schwartz, *Overload: Finding the Truth in Today's Deluge of News* [New York: Rowman & Littlefield, 2017]), pollster Peter Hart uses an example of wine, in this instance to say that mixing a good bottle and a bad bottle doesn't give you something that tastes better.

154 *each of them made reasonable, but different:* Nate Cohn, "We Gave Four Good Pollsters the Same Raw Data," *New York Times*, September 20, 2016.

Chapter Twelve: Polling in the Present Tense

158 *something like 80 or 90 percent and higher:* Nate Silver, "The Media Has a Probability Problem," Fivethirtyeight.com, September 21, 2017, https://fivethirtyeight.com/features/the-media-has-a-probability-problem/; Nate Silver, *The Signal and the Noise* (New York: Penguin, 2012); and Philip E. Tetlock and Dan Gardner, *Superforecasting: The Art and Science of Prediction* (New York: Broadway Books, 2015).

160 *using the data and believing what people were saying:* Silver, *The Signal and the Noise*, xv, 65–68.

160 *probabilities are "inherently hard to grasp":* David Leonhardt, "What I Was Wrong About This Year," *New York Times*, December 24, 2017, https://www.nytimes.com/2017/12/24/opinion/2017-wrong-numbers.html.

161   *have a particularly fun explanation:* Tetlock and Gardner, *Superforecasting*, 137.

161   *"we decide based on how we expect the future":* Tetlock and Gardner, *Super-forecasting*, 1.

Chapter Thirteen: The Politics of Inequality

166   *more negative than it had been in the year 2000:* All figures from CBS News polls, 2000–2017.

167   *said only Wall Street would be helped by the bailout:* CBS News poll, 2008.

168   *top answer was the "regulators":* CBS News poll, 2009. Data in this section is from CBS News/*New York Times* poll, April 2008; CBS News polls, December 2008; January 2009; February 2 and 22, 2009; March 2009; July 2009; and March 2010.

169   *Wall Street was among the top answers for partisans of all stripes:* CBS News poll, July 2009.

169   *Only 30 percent said it was fair as it was:* CBS News poll. Data in this section is from CBS News polls, May 2011; August 2015; and October 2015.

169   *As of 2017 the top 1 percent owned nearly 39 percent of the nation's wealth:* Matt Egan, "Record Inequality: The Top 1% Controls 38.6% of America's Wealth," CNNMoney.com, September 27, 2017, http://money .cnn.com/2017/09/27/news/economy/inequality-record-top-1-percent -wealth/index.html.

169   *The Pew Research Center showed that in 2017:* Pew Research Center, "How Wealth Inequality Has Changed in the U.S. Since the Great Recession, by Race, Ethnicity and Income," November 1, 2017, http:// www.pewresearch.org/fact-tank/2017/11/01/how-wealth-inequality -has-changed-in-the-u-s-since-the-great-recession-by-race-ethnicity -and-income/.

169   *places that were already more prosperous:* Reid Wilson, "Recession, Recovery Leave Behind Suffering Communities," *The Hill*, September 26, 2017, http://thehill.com/homenews/state-watch/352478-recession-recovery -leave-behind-suffering-communities.

170   *The middle- and lower-class families had not participated:* Thomas Piketty, translated by Arthur Goldhammer, *Capital in the Twenty-first Century* (Cambridge, MA: The Belknap Press of Harvard University Press, 2014). And for a wide-ranging study on the politics of inequality in the U.S., see Larry M. Bartels, *Unequal Democracy: The Political Economy of the New Gilded Age* (Princeton: Princeton University Press, 2008).

170   *From 1991 to 2010 the proportion of U.S. adults:* Pew Research Center, "How Wealth Inequality Has Changed in the U.S. Since the Great Recession, by Race, Ethnicity and Income." See also Pew Research Center, December 9, 2015, "The American Middle Class Is Losing Ground": http://www.pewsocialtrends.org/2015/12/09/the-american-middle -class-is-losing-ground/ and Nelson Schwartz, "Middle Class Contracted in U.S. Over 2 Decades," *New York Times*, April 24, 2017: https://www .nytimes.com/2017/04/24/business/economy/middle-class-united -states-europe-pew.html.

170   *percent majority of voters had said the U.S. economy favored the wealthy:* CBS News national exit poll 2014.

170   *In our polling, by 2015 people under forty-five:* CBS News poll. CBS News polls, August 2010; February 2015; May 2015; CBS News/*New York Times* poll, July 2016.

170   *59 percent said the U.S. economy was unfair:* CBS News Nation Tracker study, January to April 2017.

171   *in the Iowa caucuses that opened the nominating season:* CBS News Iowa Caucuses exit poll, 2012.

171   *who won lower-income voters in Michigan and Ohio:* CBS News exit polls, 2012.

171   *one-third of Republican voters:* CBS News 2012 national exit poll.

172   *the percentage saying the economy favored the wealthy jumped:* CBS News 2014 national exit poll.

172   *79 percent of those who backed Obama that year:* CBS News national exit polls, 2012.

172   *only among people who consider themselves upper- or upper-middle-class does a majority believe the economy works fairly:* CBS News Polls; CBS News Nation Tracker surveys, January to April 2017.

172 *fewer than half of Americans think either one of them:* CBS News poll, October 2017.

173 *even more so than saying they believe Democrats favor the poor:* CBS News poll, October 2017.

173 *congressional Democrats represented more of the wealthiest:* CBS News Election Unit analysis of U.S. Census Income and Housing data.

174 *he beat Clinton by nearly 30 points:* CBS News 2016 New Hampshire Democratic Primary exit poll.

174 *Wall Street hurts the economy more than it helps:* CBS News Nation Tracker recruitment survey, 2017.

174 *one-third still said the economy was unfair:* CBS News Nation Tracker survey, 2017.

177 *same patterns were true among independents and among Democrats:* CBS News Nation Tracker survey, 2017.

Chapter Fourteen: Would You Invite a Democrat to Dinner?

180 *still supporting him that summer:* It was 24 percent in July 1974. Gallup Organization, Gallup Poll (AIPO), July 1974 [survey question]; USGALLUP.911.Q01, Gallup Organization [producer]; Cornell University, Ithaca, New York, Roper Center for Public Opinion Research, iPOLL [distributor], accessed February 17, 2018.

180 *Old surveys used to ask respondents:* For example: National Opinion Research Center, University of Chicago, NORC SRS-Amalgam, December 1963 [survey question]; USNORC.SRS330.QS27, National Opinion Research Center, University of Chicago [producer]; Cornell University, Ithaca, New York, Roper Center for Public Opinion Research, iPOLL [distributor], accessed February 16, 2018. And National Opinion Research Center, University of Chicago. General Social Survey 1985, February 1985 [survey question], USNORC.GSS85.R123, National Opinion Research Center, University of Chicago [producer], Cornell University, Ithaca, New York, Roper Center for Public Opinion Research, iPOLL [distributor], accessed February 16, 2018.

182   *completely and utterly different from yours:* There is an abundance of political science literature on how people see themselves belonging to parties and partisanship; see Donald Green, Bradley Palmquist, and Eric Schickler, *Partisan Hearts and Minds: Political Parties and the Social Identities of Voters* (New Haven, CT: Yale University Press, 2002). For an alternative look at the idea of a culture war or related ideas of polarization, see Morris P. Fiorina, *Culture War? The Myth of a Polarized America* (New York: Pearson Longman, 2006).

183   *The etymology traces to Election Night television:* Ron Elving, "The Color of Politics: How Did Red and Blue States Come to Be?," NPR, November 13, 2014.

183   *spiked after 2000 and in the run-up to the 2004 contest:* Andrew Gelman, *Red State, Blue State, Rich State, Poor State: Why Americans Vote the Way They Do* (Princeton, NJ: Princeton University Press, 2008).

183   *number of Americans living in these "landslide counties":* See Bill Bishop, *The Big Sort* (New York: Houghton Mifflin, 2008). Also see "The Divide Between Red and Blue America Grew Even Deeper in 2016," *New York Times* interactive map, November 10, 2016, https://www.nytimes.com /interactive/2016/11/10/us/politics/red-blue-divide-grew-stronger-in -2016.html.

184   Applebee's America *described the "exit ramp" communities:* Doug Sosnik, Matthew Dowd, and Ron Fournier, *Applebee's America* (New York: Simon & Schuster, 2006). Political scientist Andrew Gelman pointed out that affluence mattered in the blue states, too, with "middle and upper-income voters who drive the political culture war." Andrew Gelman, *Red State, Blue State, Rich State, Poor State: Why Americans Vote the Way They Do.*

184   *"people use space as a mental shortcut":* Ryan D. Enos, *The Space Between Us* (Cambridge, UK: Cambridge University Press, 2017).

184   *They make for a functioning democracy in the first place:* See Robert D. Putnam, *Bowling Alone: The Collapse and Revival of American Community* (New York: Simon & Schuster, 2000).

185   *overall trend line from the decades now shows liberals:* CBS News poll trends, 1980–2018.

185 *who share a common view for themselves:* A raft of studies have measured polarization differently and come up with similar kinds of findings. Political science literature around the idea of partisanship polarization and how partisans see each other and how they vote is extensive. For some recommended readings, see Alan Abramowitz, *The Disappearing Center* (New Haven, CT: Yale University Press, 2010); Russell J. Dalton, *The Apartisan American* (Thousand Oaks, CA: Sage Publications, 2013); Gelman, *Red State, Blue State, Rich State, Poor State*; and John B. Judis and Ruy Teixeira, *The Emerging Democratic Majority* (New York: Scribner, 2002).

185 *negative views in the high-80-percent range:* Courtesy of my colleague Jen De Pinto, CBS News poll analysis, 2018.

186 *What struck me was getting so few policy-related answers:* CBS News and CBS News/*New York Times* poll, March 2006.

187 *I started asking division questions:* Data in this section from CBS News Nation Tracker survey, and Nation Tracker polls, January–April 2017.

191 *political scientists call negative partisanship:* See Jonathan Ladd, "Negative Partisanship May Be the Most Toxic form of Polarization," https://www.vox.com/mischiefs-of-faction/2017/6/2/15730524/negative-partisanship-toxic-polarization.

Afterword to the Paperback Edition

198 *a little over one in five Americans, at 22 percent:* CBS News Nation Tracker poll, February 2017.

198 *Almost all of these ardent backers felt he was doing things his own way or "shaking up" Washington, and were glad for it:* CBS News Battleground Tracker poll, February 2017.

199 *more so than that he had done things like cut their taxes:* CBS News Nation Tracker poll, January 2018.

199 *it was their identification as a Trump supporter that rated highest:* CBS News Nation Tracker polls, February 2017; March 2017; July 2017; January 2018.

199 *As it turned out, this group would by and large stay with him:* CBS News Nation Tracker polls, February 2017; March 2017; July 2017; January 2018; May 2018.

200 *even as the economy was seen as doing well in the minds of most Americans, this group did not become supporters:* CBS News Nation Tracker polls, February 2017; March 2017; July 2017; January 2018; May 2018.

200 *and they described their feelings at the start as angry and pessimistic:* CBS News Nation Tracker poll, February 2017. For more, see also Anthony Salvanto et al., "Does Trump Support Have a Ceiling or a Floor?," CBS News.com, February 12, 2017, https://www.cbsnews.com/news/nation -tracker-poll-does-trump-support-have-a-ceiling-or-a-floor/.

200 *and 68 percent gave the president's policies credit for that:* CBS News Nation Tracker poll, May 2018.

200 *It all described a slow hardening of opposition while that initial base held, but did not grow:* CBS News Nation Tracker polls, January 2018; May 2018.

202 *"so if we know a lot about, let's say, white working class voters":* From Kabir Khanna and Anthony Salvanto, "CBS News Battleground Tracker: How Does This Model Estimate Work?," CBSNews.com, June 3, 2018, https://www.cbsnews.com/news/cbs-news-battleground-tracker-how -does-this-model-estimate-work/.

202 *Finally, we took all the district estimates together and simulated the elections, and counted how many seats each party was winning:* See also Kabir Khanna and Anthony Salvanto, "CBS News Battleground Tracker: How Does This Model Estimate Work?," CBSNews.com, June 3, 2018, https:// www.cbsnews.com/news/cbs-news-battleground-tracker-how-does-this -model-estimate-work/. This project was done in collaboration with You-Gov's Data Science team, Ben Lauderdale, Jack Blumenau, Doug Rivers, and Delia Baily. The modeling approach used for this study of the U.S. 2018 House extended work that the YouGov team had developed for the United Kingdom's election in 2015. See Ben Lauderdale, Delia Bailey, Jack Blumenau, and Doug Rivers, "Model-Based Pre-Election Polling for National and Sub-National Outcomes in the US and UK," Working Paper, 2017, http://benjaminlauderdale.net/files/papers/mrp-polling-paper.pdf.

And for more on the technique generally, also see writings by Andrew Gelman, e.g., "Mr. P., What Is Its Secret Sauce," 2013, https://statmodeling.stat.columbia.edu/2013/10/09/mister-p-whats-its-secret-sauce/; and also, e.g., Jeffrey R. Lax and Justin Phillips, "How Should We Estimate Public Opinion in the States?," *American Journal of Political Science* 53, no. 1 (January 2009): 107–21. Also David K. Park, Andrew Gelman, and Joseph Bafumi, "Bayesian Multilevel Estimation with Poststratification: State-Level Estimates from National Polls," *Political Analysis* 12, no. 4 (2004), Society for Political Methodology.

202 *a larger Democratic majority as voters increasingly made their decisions:* CBS News Battleground Tracker poll, June 2018.

202 *while those without degrees were going for the Republican 42–35:* CBS News Battleground Tracker poll, June 2018.

203 *with independent women at 53 percent disapproval:* CBS News Battleground Tracker poll, August 2018.

203 *while three-fourths of Republicans said they needed to be punished:* CBS News Nation Tracker poll, June 2018.

203 *which at the time seemed an important factor given the Democrats' dependence on turning out less frequent voters:* CBS News Nation Tracker poll, June 2018.

204 *they felt the Republicans were working against the interests of women:* CBS News Battleground Tracker polls, August 2018; September 2018.

204 *in House contests the president was not on the ballot, but he was on voters' minds:* CBS News National Exit poll, November 2018. See also Jennifer De Pinto, "The Year in Polling 2018," CBSNews.com, December 24, 2018, https://www.cbsnews.com/news/2018-the-year-in-polling-cbs-news/.

205 *a range of possibilities in reporting poll information around campaigns:* CBS News Battleground Tracker estimate, October 2018.

205 *If that happened, we reported, it would mean Democrats would fall just short in their bid for the majority:* CBS News Battleground Tracker estimate, October 2018.

206 *for a high scenario of 232:* CBS News Battleground Tracker estimate, November 2018.

206   *with a jump of more than 30 million from the last midterm:* Voter turn-out data from CBS News elections results; Edison Media Research. And see Michael McDonald, United States Elections Project, http://www .electproject.org/. See also Grace Segers, "Record Voter Turnout in 2018 Midterm Elections." November 7, 2018. CBSNews.com, https://www .cbsnews.com/news/record-voter-turnout-in-2018-midterm-elections/.

206   *and these voters picked Democrats 62–36:* CBS News National Exit poll, November 2018.

206   *and three-quarters of those who'd only said that they "probably" would:* You-Gov post-election recontact study shared with the author, November 2018.

206   *than Republican candidates did in drawing over Hillary Clinton voters (5 percent):* CBS News National Exit poll, November 2018.

207   *was about what our pre-election estimates had suggested:* It had been 6 percent Trump-to-Democratic and 3 percent Clinton-to-Republican. CBS News Battleground Tracker poll, November 2018; https://www.cbsnews .com/news/house-democrats-in-position-to-gain-but-still-face-hurdles -cbs-news-poll/.

209   *who'd led or tied for a party's lead in those kinds of national CBS News polls across the last four presidential cycles:* Analysis of CBS News and CBS News/*New York Times* polls, 1999, 2000, 2003, 2004, 2007, 2008, 2011, 2012, 2015, 2016. And see Fred Backus, "The Democratic Primary: How Much Does Being an Early Frontrunner Matter?," CBS News. com, March 6, 2019, https://www.cbsnews.com/news/the-democratic -primary-how-much-does-being-an-early-frontrunner-matter/.

211   *had been right (46 percent) more than wrong (19 percent), while another third were not sure:* YouGov post-election recontact study, November 2018.

Index